A WHO HQ GRAPHIC

Who Is Tibet's Exiled Leader?

THE 14TH DALAI LAMA

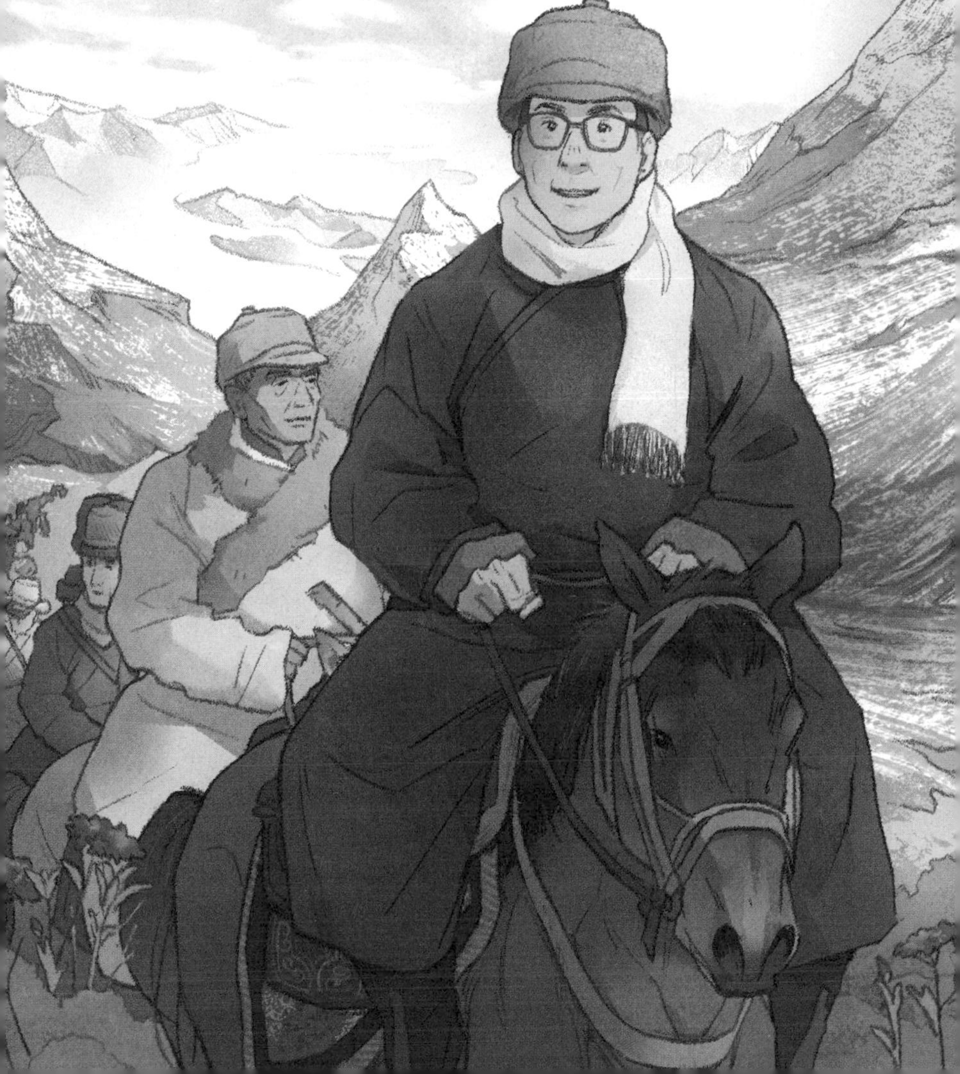

To Natascha Morris who turned me from reader to writer
in the GN realm, and to Rachel Sonis for her incredible
patience and kindness in guiding me through that realm—TR

To EC, FG, WS, and my mom—AP

PENGUIN WORKSHOP
An imprint of Penguin Random House LLC, New York

First published in the United States of America by Penguin Workshop,
an imprint of Penguin Random House LLC, New York, 2023

Visit us online at penguinrandomhouse.com.

Library of Congress Cataloging-in-Publication Data is available.

Manufactured in Italy

ISBN 9780593384589 (pbk)   10 9 8 7 6 5 4 3 2 1 LEG
ISBN 9780593384602 (hc)   10 9 8 7 6 5 4 3 2 1 LEG

Lettering by Comicraft
Design by Jay Emmanuel

This is a work of nonfiction. All of the events that unfold in the narrative
are rooted in historical fact. Some dialogue and characters have been fictionalized
in order to illustrate or teach a historical point.

For more information about your favorite historical figures, places, and events,
please visit whohq.com.

A WHO HQ GRAPHIC NOVEL

Who Is Tibet's Exiled Leader?
THE 14TH DALAI LAMA

by Teresa Robeson
illustrated by Angela Poon

Penguin Workshop

Introduction

In the spring of 1959, thousands of Tibetans flocked to Lhasa, the capital city of Tibet, for Monlam Chenmo, the Great Prayer Festival, and to catch a glimpse of their beloved leader, the Dalai Lama. The Precious Protector, as he was often called, was set to make his usual public appearance during the celebration.

At just twenty-three years old, the Dalai Lama might seem a bit young to be the leader of six million Tibetan people. But it's a role he was born into: The Dalai Lama (born Lhamo Thondup) had held the "job" of spiritual leader since he was four, and was officially crowned political leader at fifteen. In fact, at the time of the festival, he was in the middle of finishing up his final exams for his doctorate degree in Buddhist Studies at Lhasa's Jokhang Temple—a joyous conclusion of his studies for the highest monastic degree.

The problem was that this year's Monlam wasn't quite as joyous. Tibetans had been upset ever since 1950 when Communist leader Chairman Mao Zedong in neighboring China sent the People's Liberation Army (PLA) across the border to occupy Tibetan towns. China claimed that Tibet used to be a part of China and should be again. They forced Tibetan officials to sign a document called the "Seventeen-Point Agreement," which granted China the right to rule Tibet. Tibetans, however, didn't want to be ruled by a foreign government, and protesters fought back in towns near the Eastern border. In fact, many Tibetans from that region also fled the fighting and came to Lhasa in fear and outrage.

Tensions were running high. The PLA had headquarters right outside of the capital city, and the thousands of citizens gathering within Lhasa for the festival felt angry and nervous about what would happen next to their country. Because of this, the Dalai Lama's chief of security, Phuntsog Tashi Taklha, decided it would be safer for the Dalai Lama to skip the festival and remain inside the Jokhang Temple during his exams. So he announced that the Precious Protector was feeling unwell and wouldn't appear in public. At the same time, the Chinese government sent the Dalai Lama an invitation to attend a dance troupe performance at their headquarters after his exams. These two incidents sparked rumors and fears among Tibetans that the Dalai Lama's life was in danger.

The Monlam festival ended on March 4, and it was time for the Dalai Lama to return home to the Norbulingka Palace in the usual splendid procession. Seeing him parading through the streets settled the crowd for a time, though that wouldn't last for very long.

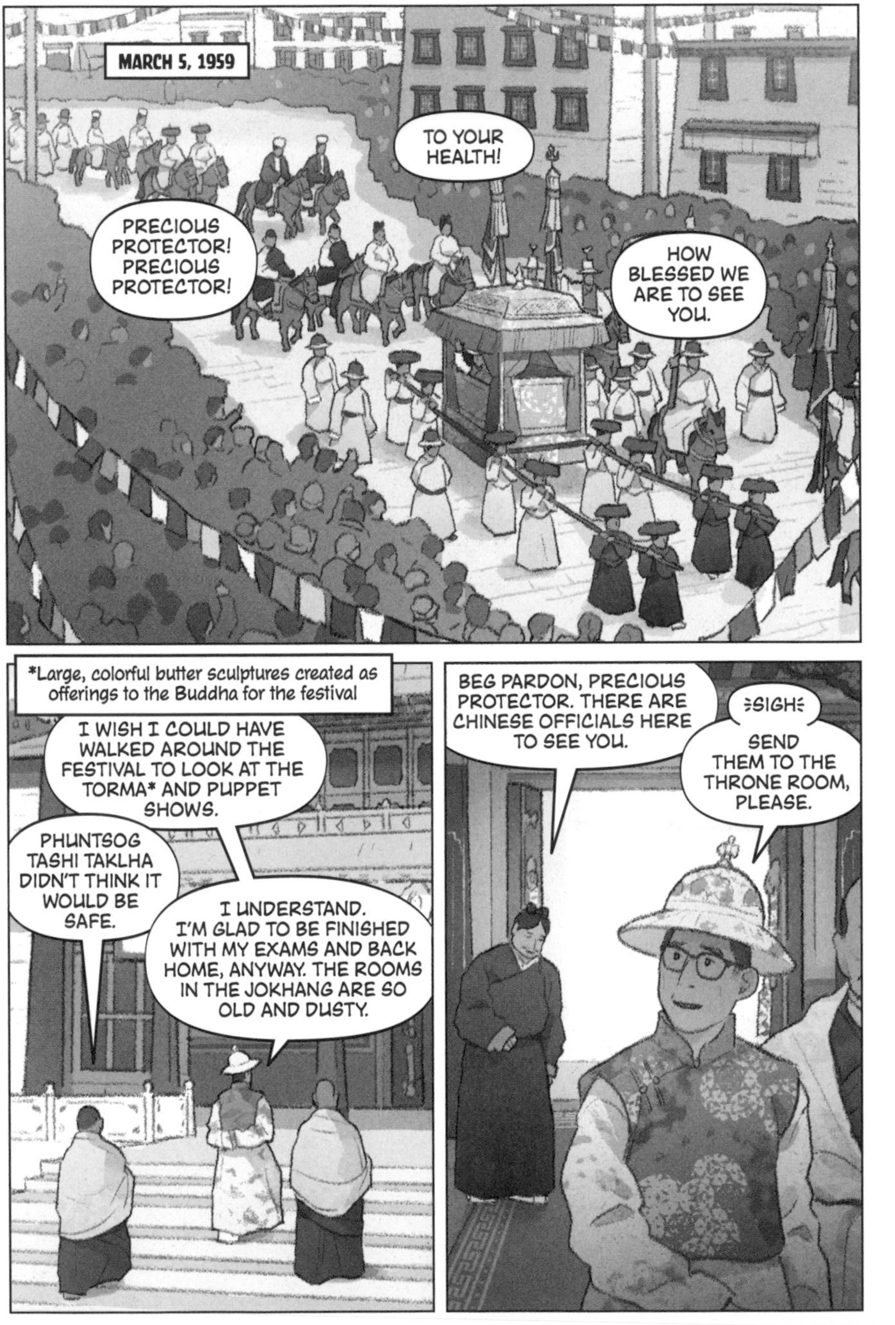
MARCH 5, 1959
TO YOUR HEALTH!
PRECIOUS PROTECTOR! PRECIOUS PROTECTOR!
HOW BLESSED WE ARE TO SEE YOU.
*Large, colorful butter sculptures created as offerings to the Buddha for the festival
I WISH I COULD HAVE WALKED AROUND THE FESTIVAL TO LOOK AT THE TORMA* AND PUPPET SHOWS.
PHUNTSOG TASHI TAKLHA DIDN'T THINK IT WOULD BE SAFE.
I UNDERSTAND. I'M GLAD TO BE FINISHED WITH MY EXAMS AND BACK HOME, ANYWAY. THE ROOMS IN THE JOKHANG ARE SO OLD AND DUSTY.
BEG PARDON, PRECIOUS PROTECTOR. THERE ARE CHINESE OFFICIALS HERE TO SEE YOU.
SIGH
SEND THEM TO THE THRONE ROOM, PLEASE.

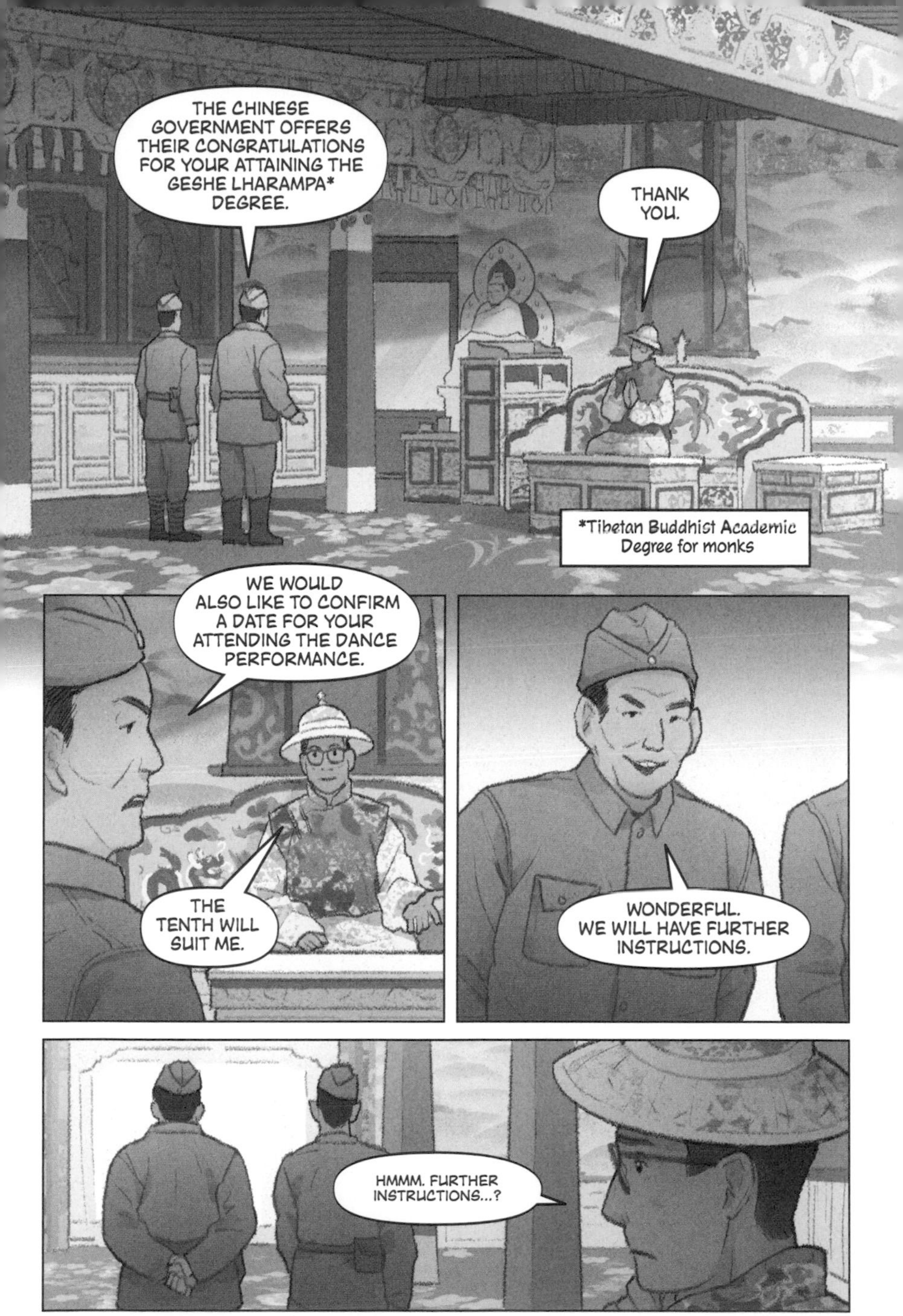
THE CHINESE GOVERNMENT OFFERS THEIR CONGRATULATIONS FOR YOUR ATTAINING THE GESHE LHARAMPA* DEGREE.
THANK YOU.
*Tibetan Buddhist Academic Degree for monks
WE WOULD ALSO LIKE TO CONFIRM A DATE FOR YOUR ATTENDING THE DANCE PERFORMANCE.
THE TENTH WILL SUIT ME.
WONDERFUL. WE WILL HAVE FURTHER INSTRUCTIONS.
HMMM. FURTHER INSTRUCTIONS...?

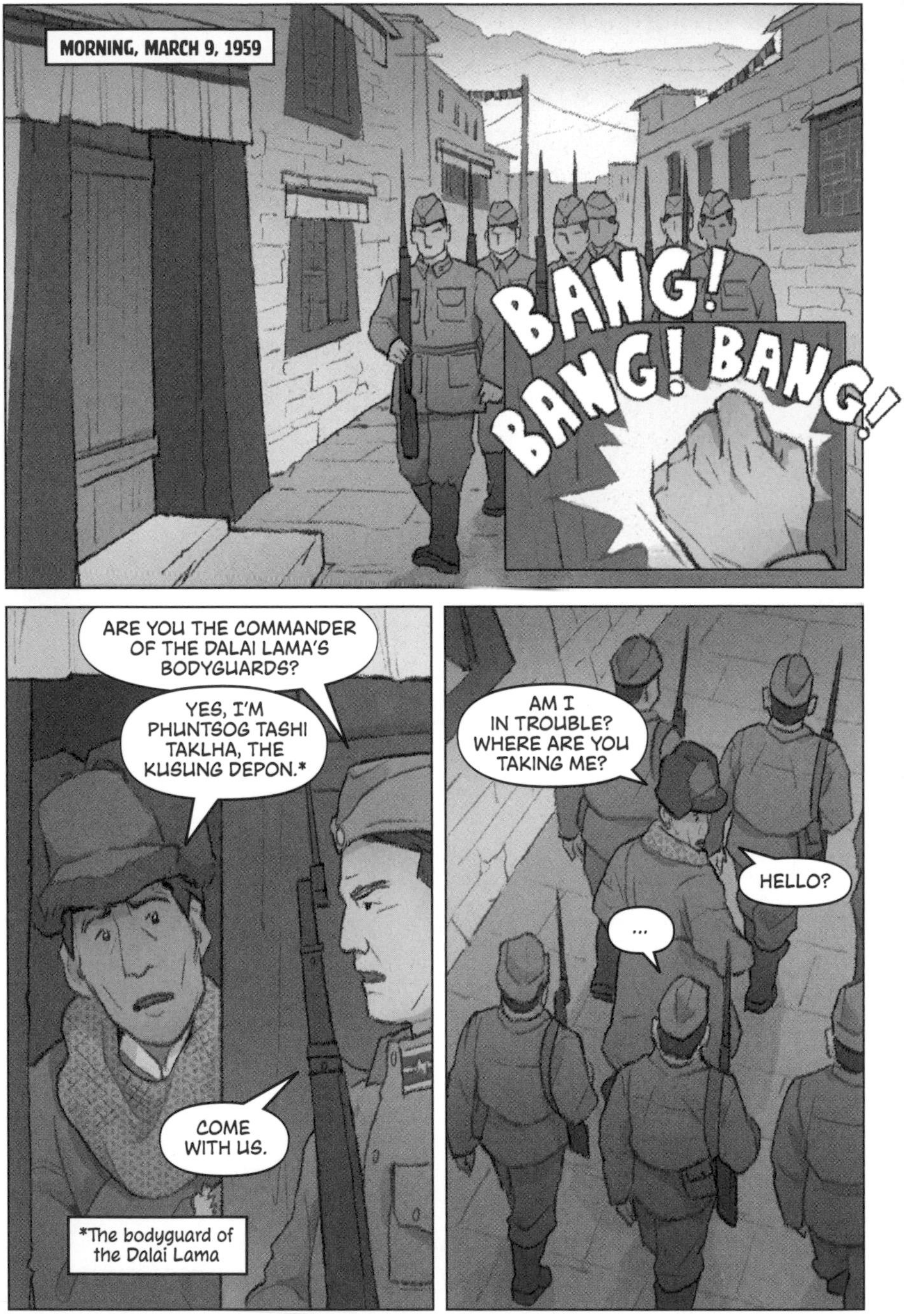
MORNING, MARCH 9, 1959
BANG! BANG! BANG!
ARE YOU THE COMMANDER OF THE DALAI LAMA'S BODYGUARDS?
YES, I'M PHUNTSOG TASHI TAKLHA, THE KUSUNG DEPON.*
COME WITH US.
*The bodyguard of the Dalai Lama
AM I IN TROUBLE? WHERE ARE YOU TAKING ME?
HELLO?
...

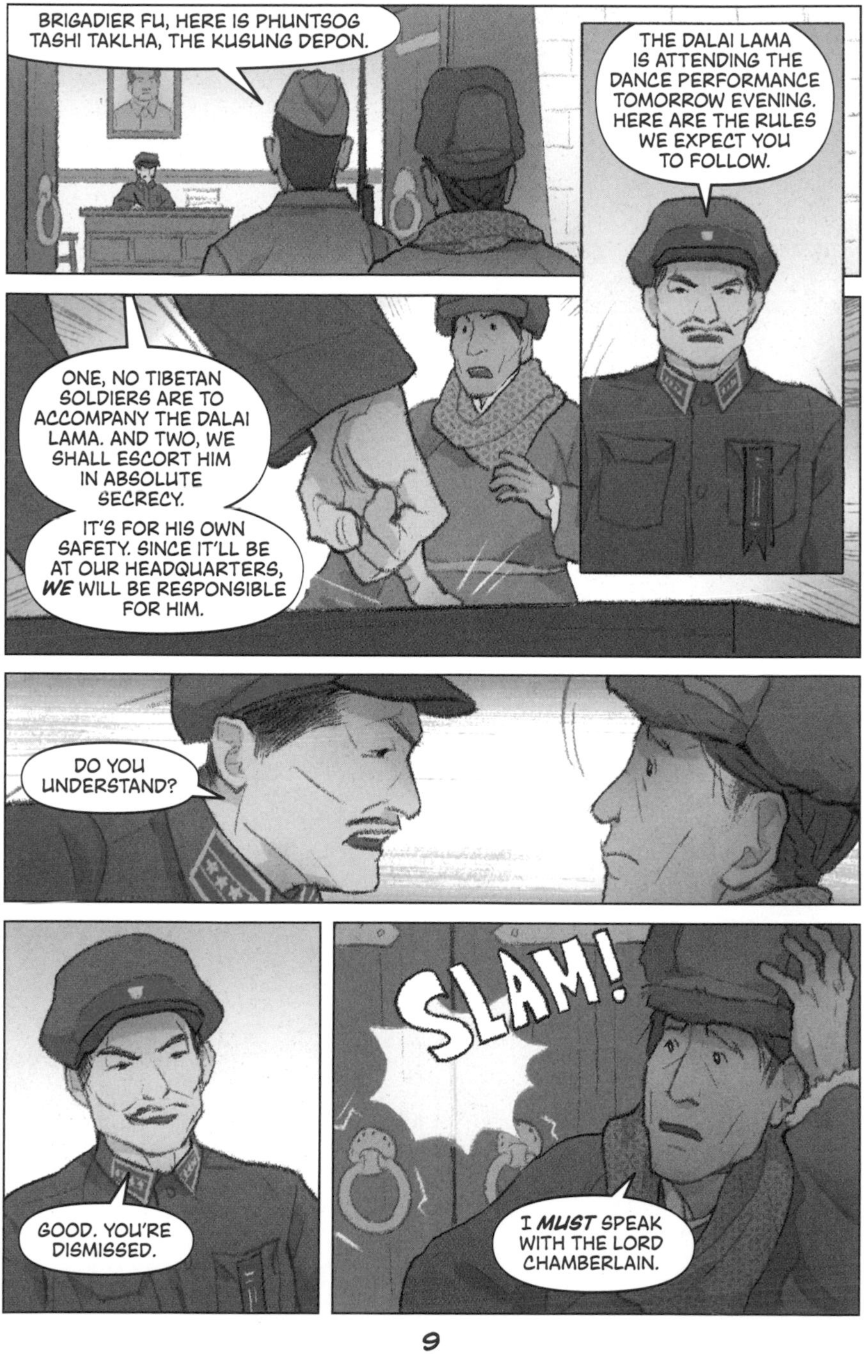
BRIGADIER FU, HERE IS PHUNTSOG TASHI TAKLHA, THE KUSUNG DEPON.
THE DALAI LAMA IS ATTENDING THE DANCE PERFORMANCE TOMORROW EVENING. HERE ARE THE RULES WE EXPECT YOU TO FOLLOW.
ONE, NO TIBETAN SOLDIERS ARE TO ACCOMPANY THE DALAI LAMA. AND TWO, WE SHALL ESCORT HIM IN ABSOLUTE SECRECY.
IT'S FOR HIS OWN SAFETY. SINCE IT'LL BE AT OUR HEADQUARTERS, ***WE*** WILL BE RESPONSIBLE FOR HIM.
DO YOU UNDERSTAND?
GOOD. YOU'RE DISMISSED.
SLAM!
I ***MUST*** SPEAK WITH THE LORD CHAMBERLAIN.

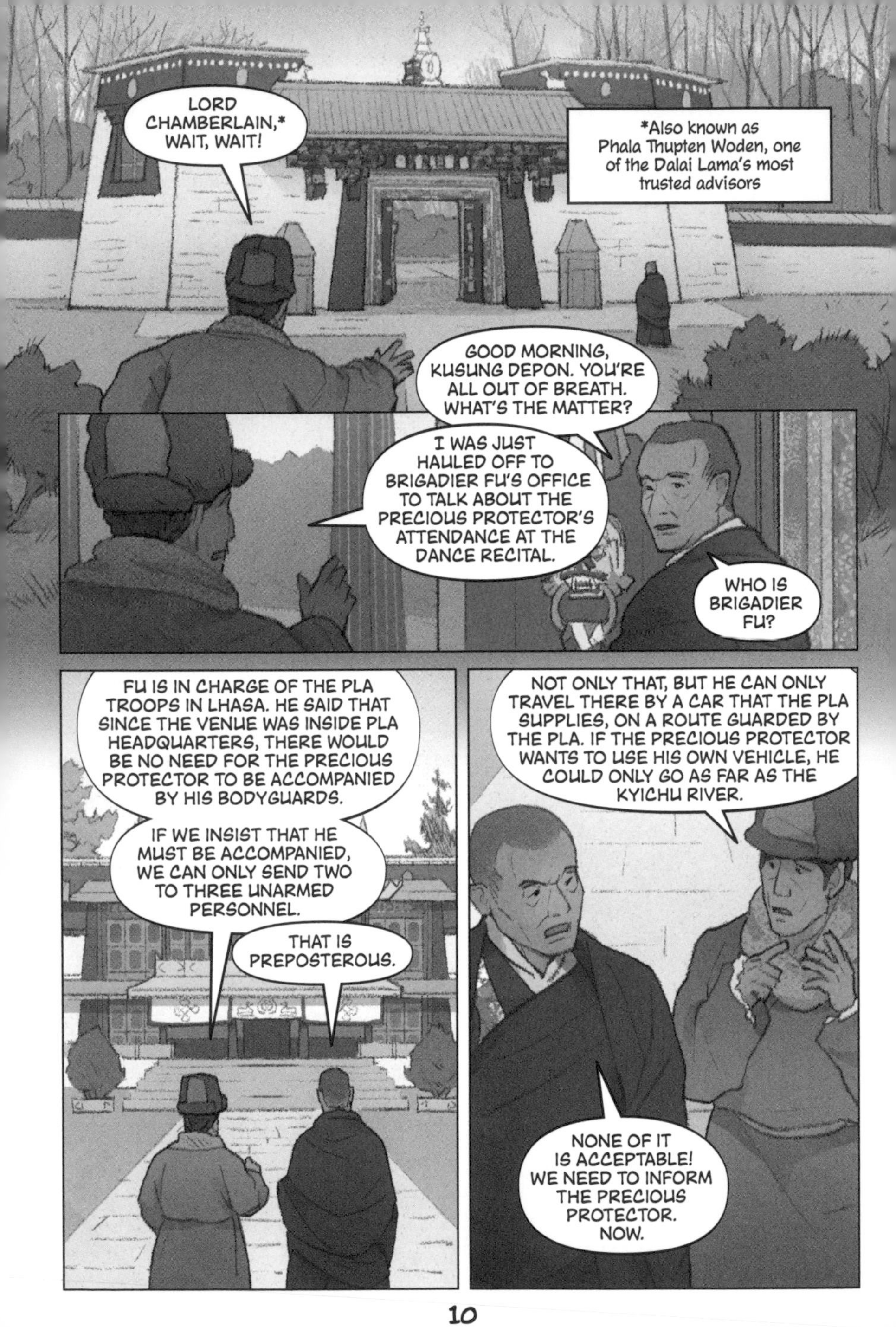
LORD CHAMBERLAIN,* WAIT, WAIT!
*Also known as Phala Thupten Woden, one of the Dalai Lama's most trusted advisors
GOOD MORNING, KUSUNG DEPON. YOU'RE ALL OUT OF BREATH. WHAT'S THE MATTER?
I WAS JUST HAULED OFF TO BRIGADIER FU'S OFFICE TO TALK ABOUT THE PRECIOUS PROTECTOR'S ATTENDANCE AT THE DANCE RECITAL.
WHO IS BRIGADIER FU?
FU IS IN CHARGE OF THE PLA TROOPS IN LHASA. HE SAID THAT SINCE THE VENUE WAS INSIDE PLA HEADQUARTERS, THERE WOULD BE NO NEED FOR THE PRECIOUS PROTECTOR TO BE ACCOMPANIED BY HIS BODYGUARDS.
IF WE INSIST THAT HE MUST BE ACCOMPANIED, WE CAN ONLY SEND TWO TO THREE UNARMED PERSONNEL.
THAT IS PREPOSTEROUS.
NOT ONLY THAT, BUT HE CAN ONLY TRAVEL THERE BY A CAR THAT THE PLA SUPPLIES, ON A ROUTE GUARDED BY THE PLA. IF THE PRECIOUS PROTECTOR WANTS TO USE HIS OWN VEHICLE, HE COULD ONLY GO AS FAR AS THE KYICHU RIVER.
NONE OF IT IS ACCEPTABLE! WE NEED TO INFORM THE PRECIOUS PROTECTOR. NOW.

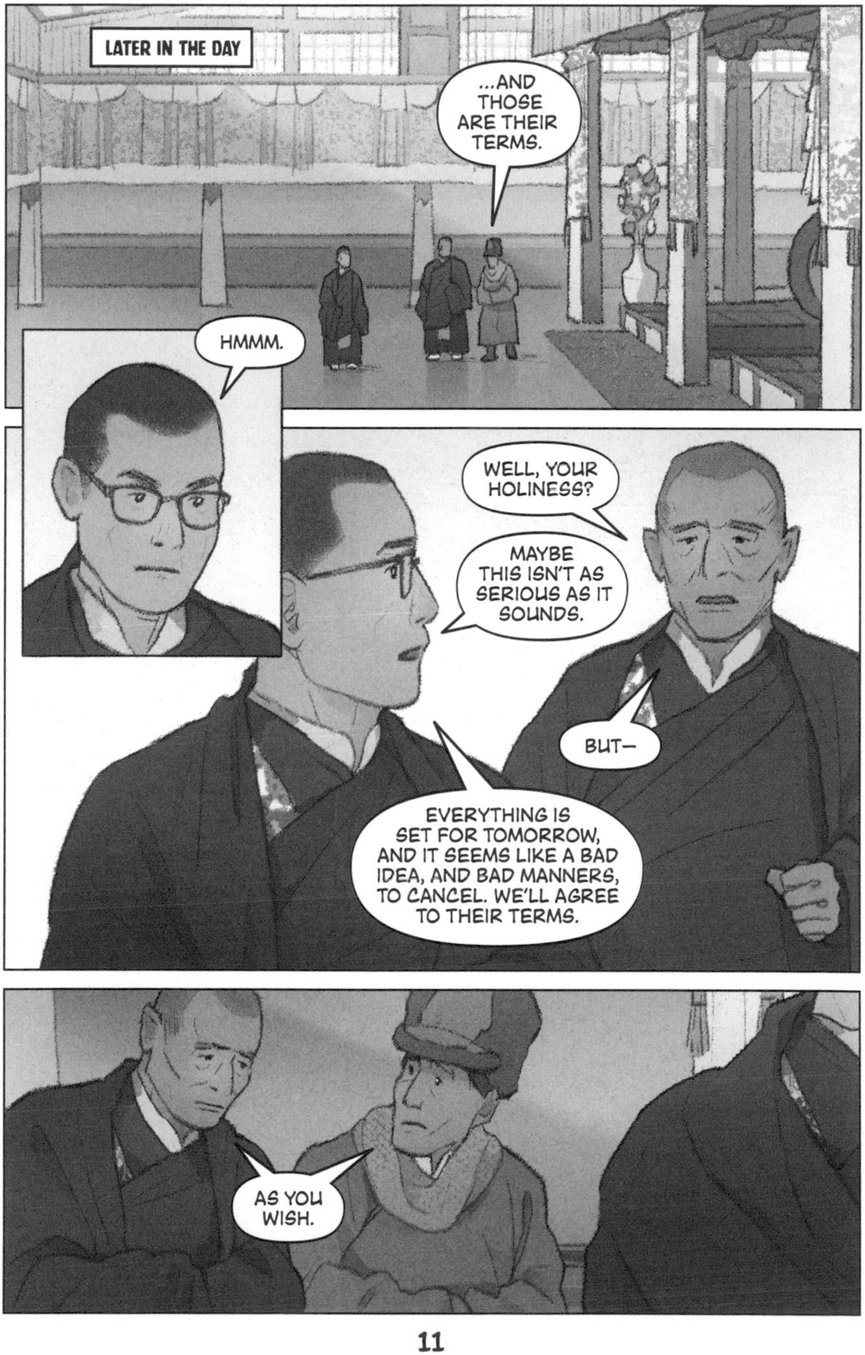
LATER IN THE DAY
...AND THOSE ARE THEIR TERMS.
HMMM.
WELL, YOUR HOLINESS?
MAYBE THIS ISN'T AS SERIOUS AS IT SOUNDS.
BUT—
EVERYTHING IS SET FOR TOMORROW, AND IT SEEMS LIKE A BAD IDEA, AND BAD MANNERS, TO CANCEL. WE'LL AGREE TO THEIR TERMS.
AS YOU WISH.

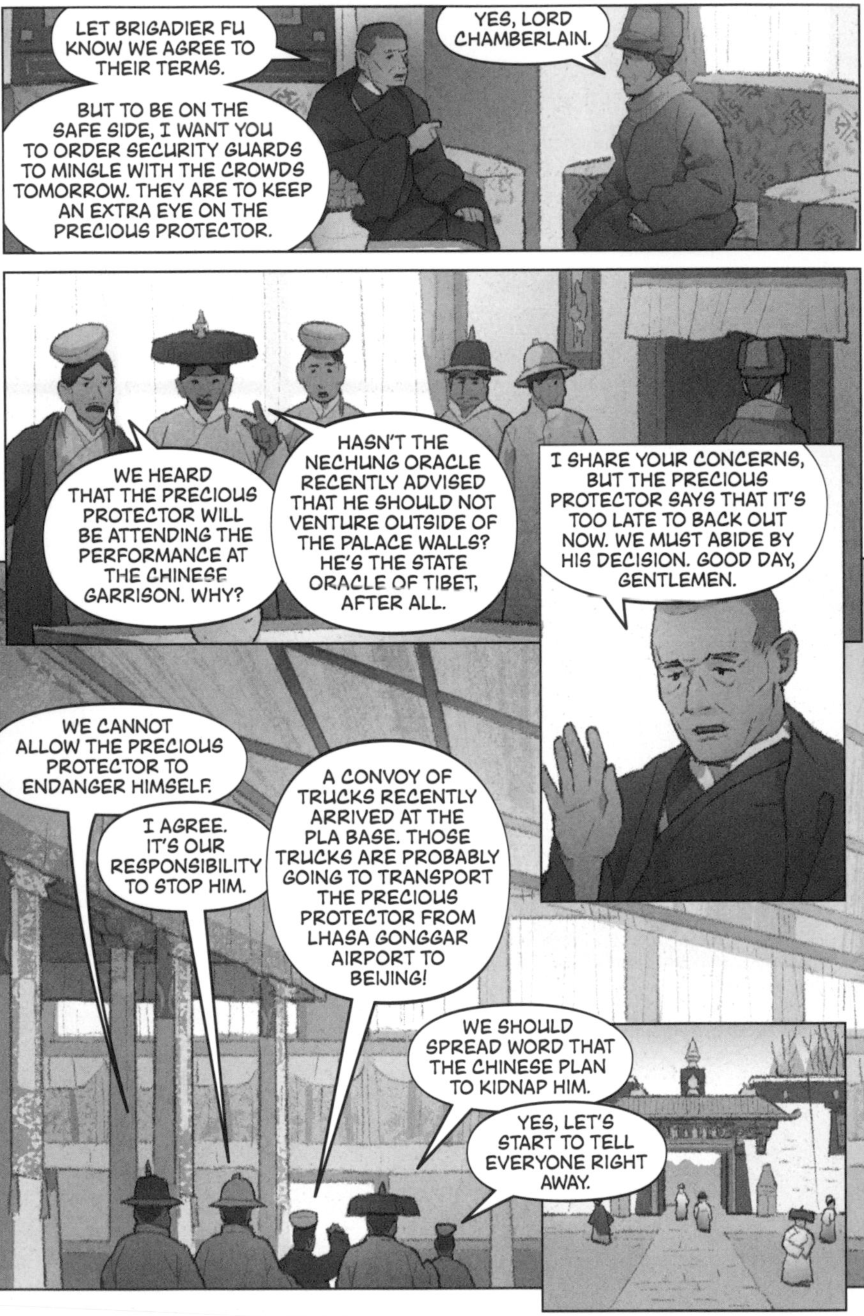
LET BRIGADIER FU KNOW WE AGREE TO THEIR TERMS.
BUT TO BE ON THE SAFE SIDE, I WANT YOU TO ORDER SECURITY GUARDS TO MINGLE WITH THE CROWDS TOMORROW. THEY ARE TO KEEP AN EXTRA EYE ON THE PRECIOUS PROTECTOR.
YES, LORD CHAMBERLAIN.
WE HEARD THAT THE PRECIOUS PROTECTOR WILL BE ATTENDING THE PERFORMANCE AT THE CHINESE GARRISON. WHY?
HASN'T THE NECHUNG ORACLE RECENTLY ADVISED THAT HE SHOULD NOT VENTURE OUTSIDE OF THE PALACE WALLS? HE'S THE STATE ORACLE OF TIBET, AFTER ALL.
I SHARE YOUR CONCERNS, BUT THE PRECIOUS PROTECTOR SAYS THAT IT'S TOO LATE TO BACK OUT NOW. WE MUST ABIDE BY HIS DECISION. GOOD DAY, GENTLEMEN.
WE CANNOT ALLOW THE PRECIOUS PROTECTOR TO ENDANGER HIMSELF.
I AGREE. IT'S OUR RESPONSIBILITY TO STOP HIM.
A CONVOY OF TRUCKS RECENTLY ARRIVED AT THE PLA BASE. THOSE TRUCKS ARE PROBABLY GOING TO TRANSPORT THE PRECIOUS PROTECTOR FROM LHASA GONGGAR AIRPORT TO BEIJING!
WE SHOULD SPREAD WORD THAT THE CHINESE PLAN TO KIDNAP HIM.
YES, LET'S START TO TELL EVERYONE RIGHT AWAY.

Tibetan Oracles

Many different cultures and religions have the concept of oracles. Usually an appointed person, such as a priest or priestess, acts as a medium that a god or goddess speaks through. People who want advice or wisdom from a divine source will consult the associated oracle. The person acting as the oracle usually goes into a mystical trance and channels the particular god who is being asked for advice.

In Tibet, the most important one is the Nechung Oracle, which has been around for hundreds of years. This oracle embodies Dorje Drakden, the protector god of Tibet and, therefore, it's the one that the Tibetan government mainly uses.

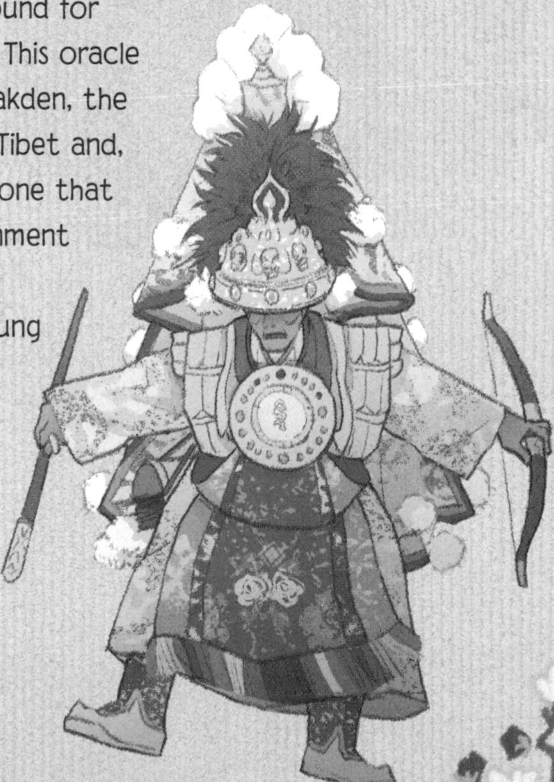

Besides the Nechung Oracle, the Dalai Lama also looks to the Gadong, Tenma, and Shugden oracles for guidance.

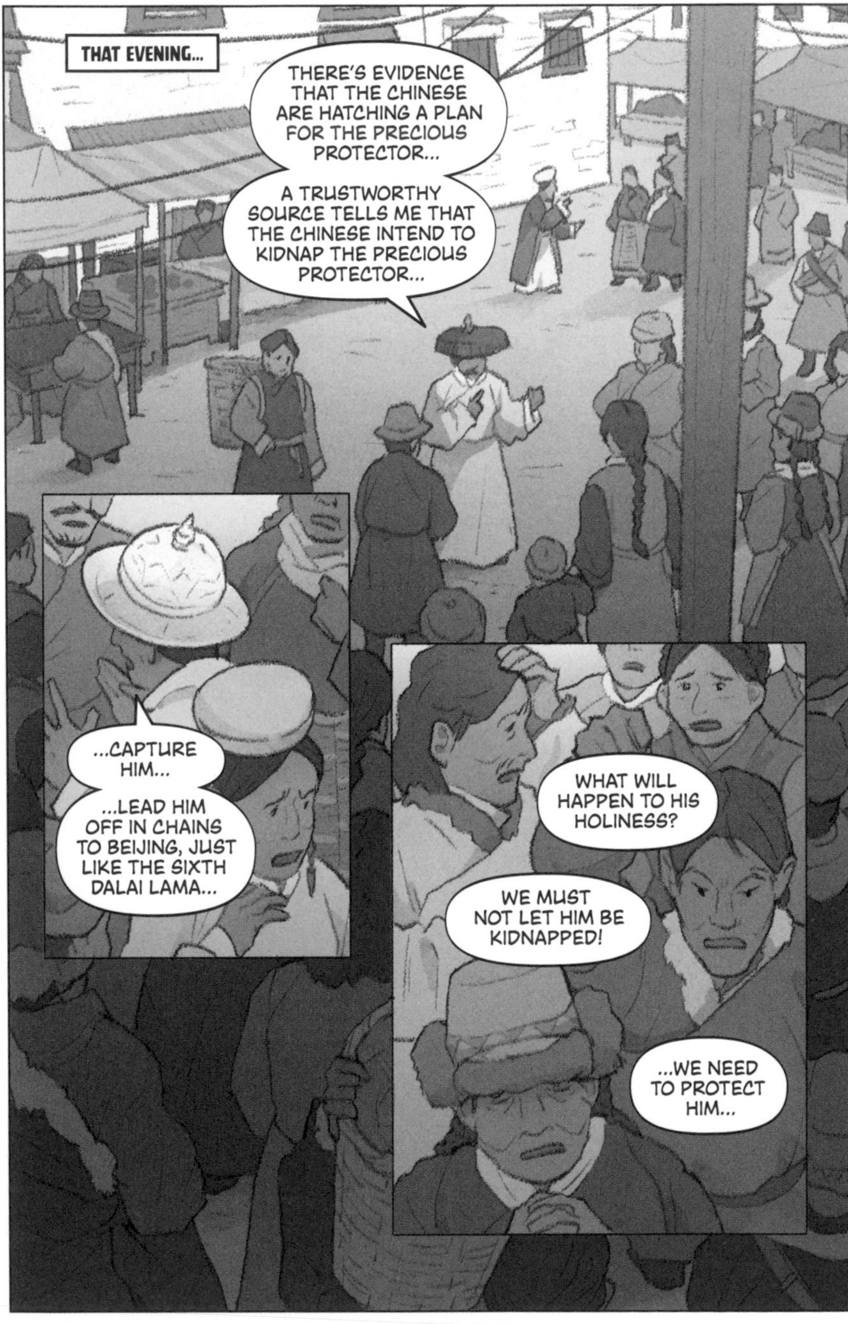
THAT EVENING...
THERE'S EVIDENCE THAT THE CHINESE ARE HATCHING A PLAN FOR THE PRECIOUS PROTECTOR...
A TRUSTWORTHY SOURCE TELLS ME THAT THE CHINESE INTEND TO KIDNAP THE PRECIOUS PROTECTOR...
...CAPTURE HIM...
...LEAD HIM OFF IN CHAINS TO BEIJING, JUST LIKE THE SIXTH DALAI LAMA...
WHAT WILL HAPPEN TO HIS HOLINESS?
WE MUST NOT LET HIM BE KIDNAPPED!
...WE NEED TO PROTECT HIM...

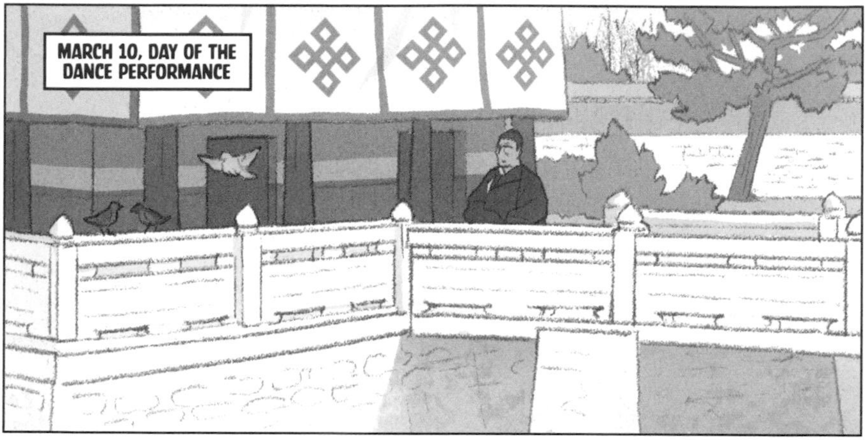
MARCH 10, DAY OF THE DANCE PERFORMANCE

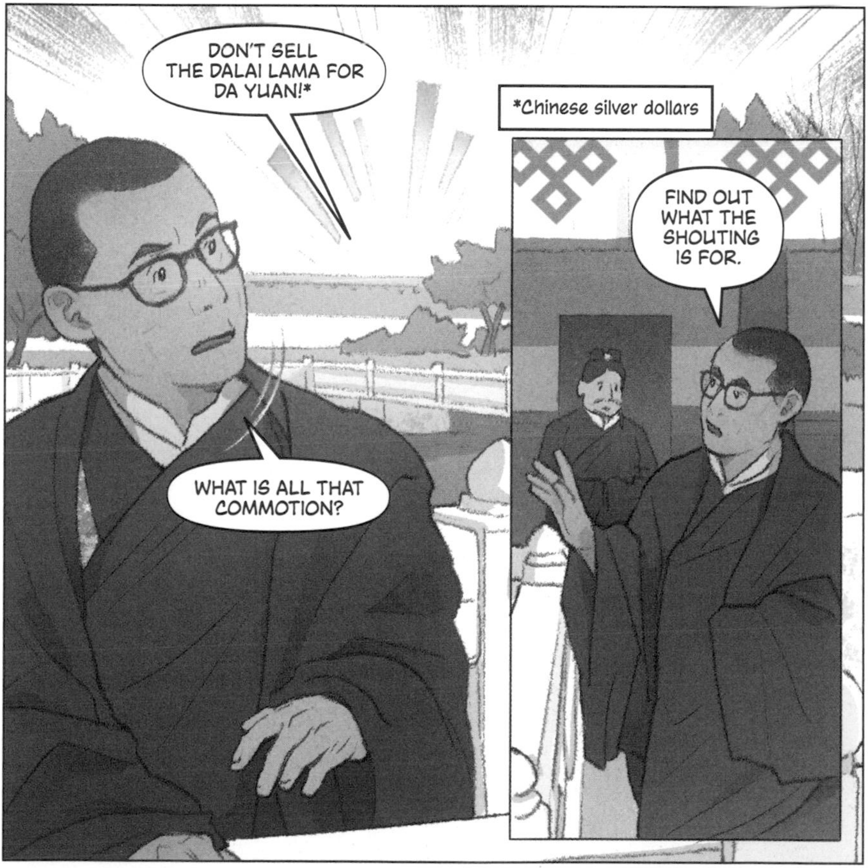
DON'T SELL THE DALAI LAMA FOR DA YUAN!*
WHAT IS ALL THAT COMMOTION?
*Chinese silver dollars
FIND OUT WHAT THE SHOUTING IS FOR.

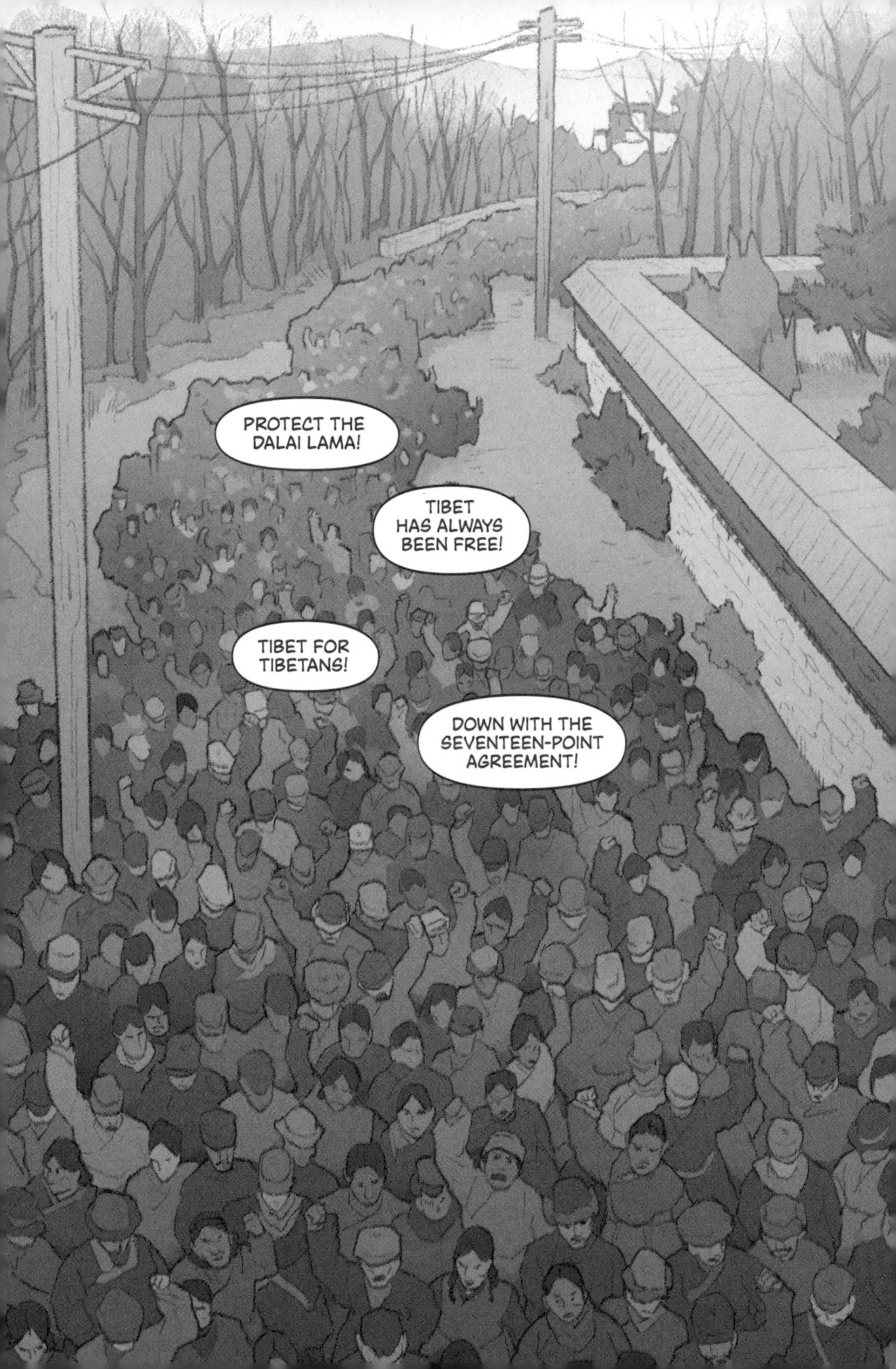
PROTECT THE DALAI LAMA!
TIBET HAS ALWAYS BEEN FREE!
TIBET FOR TIBETANS!
DOWN WITH THE SEVENTEEN-POINT AGREEMENT!

The Seventeen-Point Agreement

The "Seventeen-Point Agreement" (also known as the "Agreement of the Central People's Government and the Local Government of Tibet on Measures for the Peaceful Liberation of Tibet") was signed on May 23, 1951, by Chairman Mao Zedong. Mao believed that Tibet had been a part of China before and should be returned to its rightful owner once again. The agreement not only allowed the Chinese government to rule over Tibet, but also wanted Tibetan officials to actively assist in giving their national defense forces to the People's Liberation Army.

Tibetans have never recognized the agreement to be legitimate because, to them, Tibet had never been a part of China, and therefore could not be reabsorbed. Even though Tibetan officials were forced to sign it on May 23, 1951, Tibetans also never considered the document to be legal because the officials never brought their government seals (name stamps) with them. The seals used to stamp the document were copies made by the Chinese.

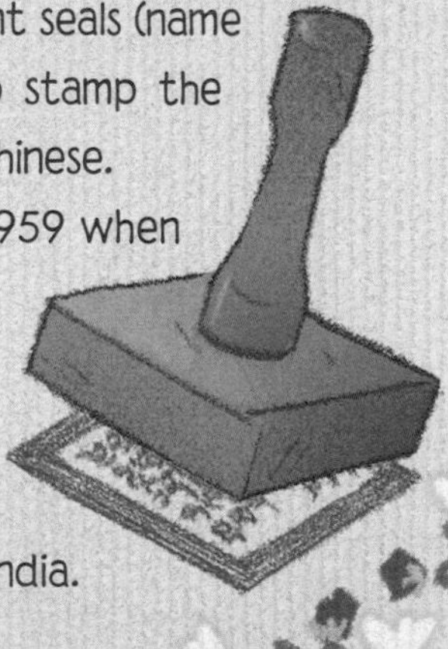

The agreement lasted until March 1959 when tens of thousands of Tibetans fought against the Chinese government. Cooperation between the two countries concluded with the Dalai Lama's escape to exile in India.

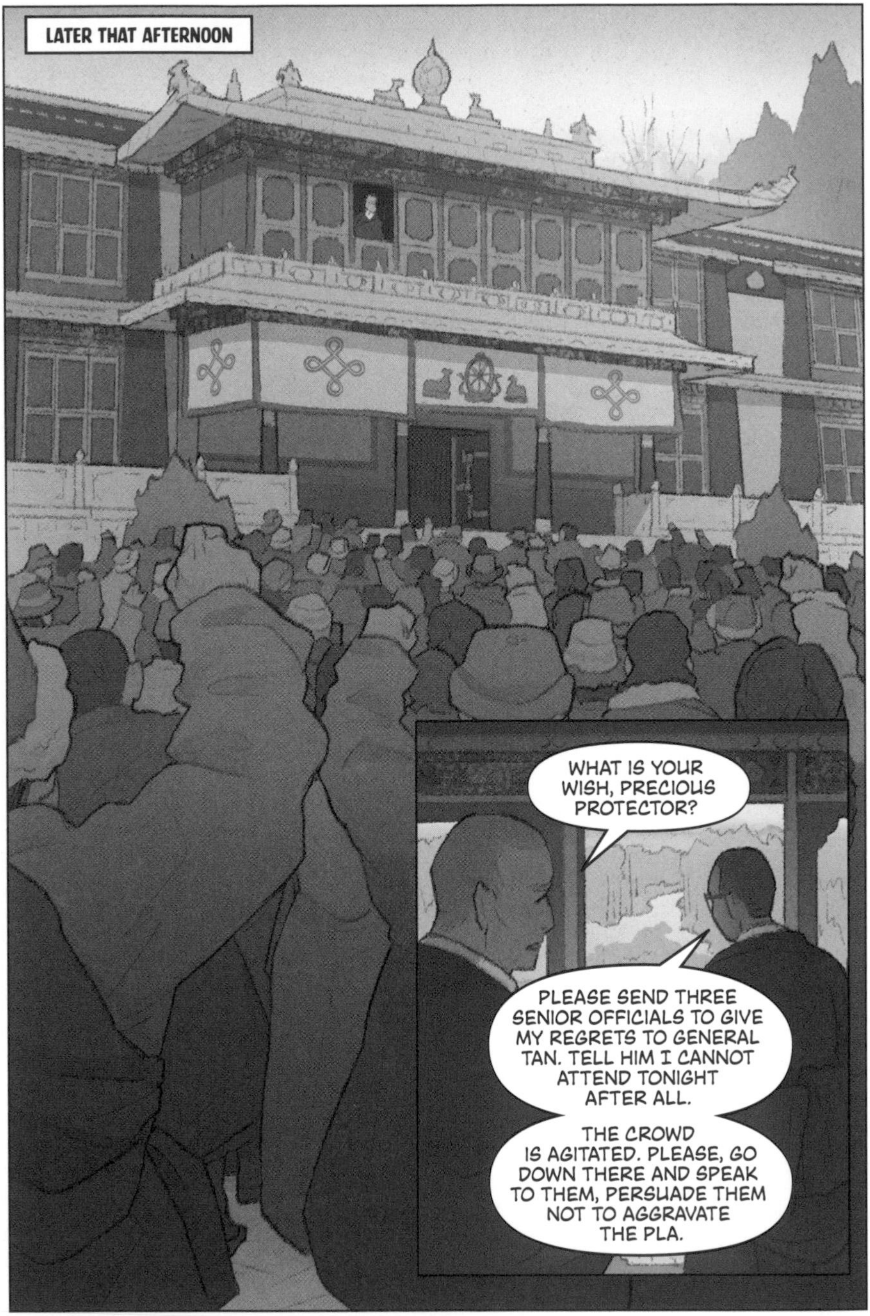
LATER THAT AFTERNOON
WHAT IS YOUR WISH, PRECIOUS PROTECTOR?
PLEASE SEND THREE SENIOR OFFICIALS TO GIVE MY REGRETS TO GENERAL TAN. TELL HIM I CANNOT ATTEND TONIGHT AFTER ALL.
THE CROWD IS AGITATED. PLEASE, GO DOWN THERE AND SPEAK TO THEM, PERSUADE THEM NOT TO AGGRAVATE THE PLA.

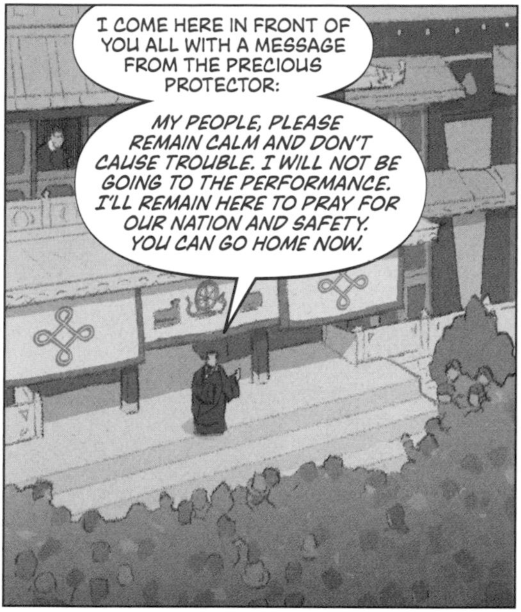
I COME HERE IN FRONT OF YOU ALL WITH A MESSAGE FROM THE PRECIOUS PROTECTOR:
MY PEOPLE, PLEASE REMAIN CALM AND DON'T CAUSE TROUBLE. I WILL NOT BE GOING TO THE PERFORMANCE. I'LL REMAIN HERE TO PRAY FOR OUR NATION AND SAFETY. YOU CAN GO HOME NOW.

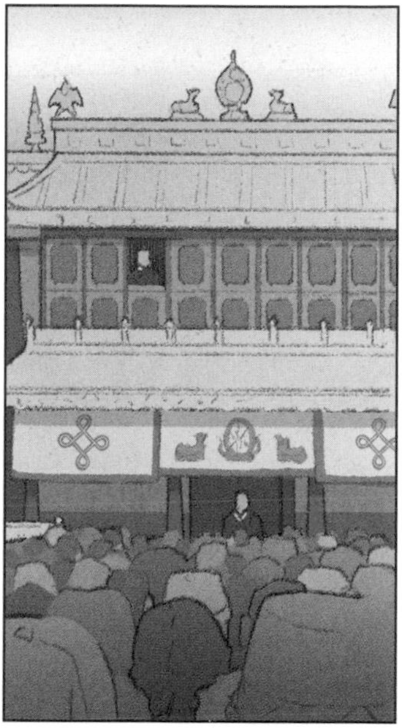

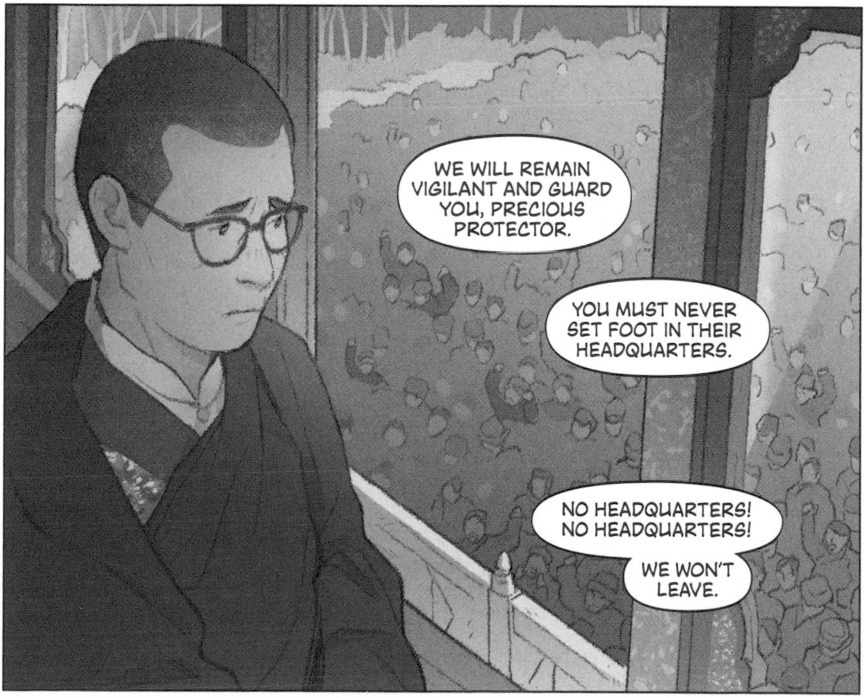
WE WILL REMAIN VIGILANT AND GUARD YOU, PRECIOUS PROTECTOR.
YOU MUST NEVER SET FOOT IN THEIR HEADQUARTERS.
NO HEADQUARTERS! NO HEADQUARTERS!
WE WON'T LEAVE.

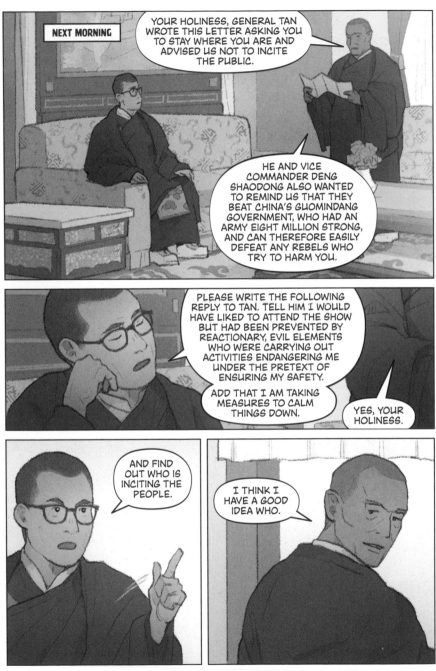

NEXT MORNING

YOUR HOLINESS, GENERAL TAN WROTE THIS LETTER ASKING YOU TO STAY WHERE YOU ARE AND ADVISED US NOT TO INCITE THE PUBLIC.

HE AND VICE COMMANDER DENG SHAODONG ALSO WANTED TO REMIND US THAT THEY BEAT CHINA'S GUOMINDANG GOVERNMENT, WHO HAD AN ARMY EIGHT MILLION STRONG, AND CAN THEREFORE EASILY DEFEAT ANY REBELS WHO TRY TO HARM YOU.

PLEASE WRITE THE FOLLOWING REPLY TO TAN. TELL HIM I WOULD HAVE LIKED TO ATTEND THE SHOW BUT HAD BEEN PREVENTED BY REACTIONARY, EVIL ELEMENTS WHO WERE CARRYING OUT ACTIVITIES ENDANGERING ME UNDER THE PRETEXT OF ENSURING MY SAFETY.

ADD THAT I AM TAKING MEASURES TO CALM THINGS DOWN.

YES, YOUR HOLINESS.

AND FIND OUT WHO IS INCITING THE PEOPLE.

I THINK I HAVE A GOOD IDEA WHO.

20

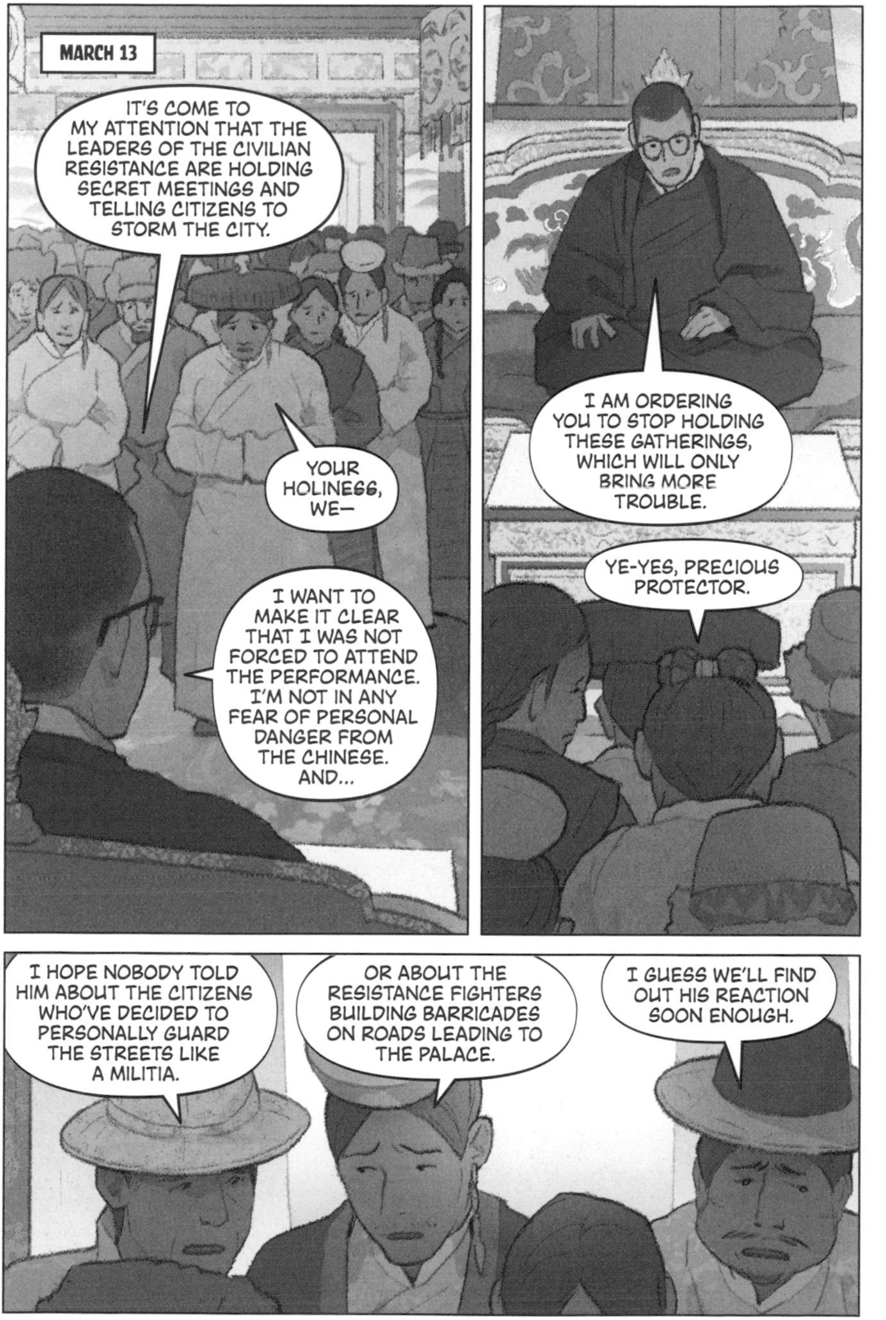
MARCH 13
IT'S COME TO MY ATTENTION THAT THE LEADERS OF THE CIVILIAN RESISTANCE ARE HOLDING SECRET MEETINGS AND TELLING CITIZENS TO STORM THE CITY.
YOUR HOLINESS, WE—
I WANT TO MAKE IT CLEAR THAT I WAS NOT FORCED TO ATTEND THE PERFORMANCE. I'M NOT IN ANY FEAR OF PERSONAL DANGER FROM THE CHINESE. AND...
I AM ORDERING YOU TO STOP HOLDING THESE GATHERINGS, WHICH WILL ONLY BRING MORE TROUBLE.
YE-YES, PRECIOUS PROTECTOR.
I HOPE NOBODY TOLD HIM ABOUT THE CITIZENS WHO'VE DECIDED TO PERSONALLY GUARD THE STREETS LIKE A MILITIA.
OR ABOUT THE RESISTANCE FIGHTERS BUILDING BARRICADES ON ROADS LEADING TO THE PALACE.
I GUESS WE'LL FIND OUT HIS REACTION SOON ENOUGH.

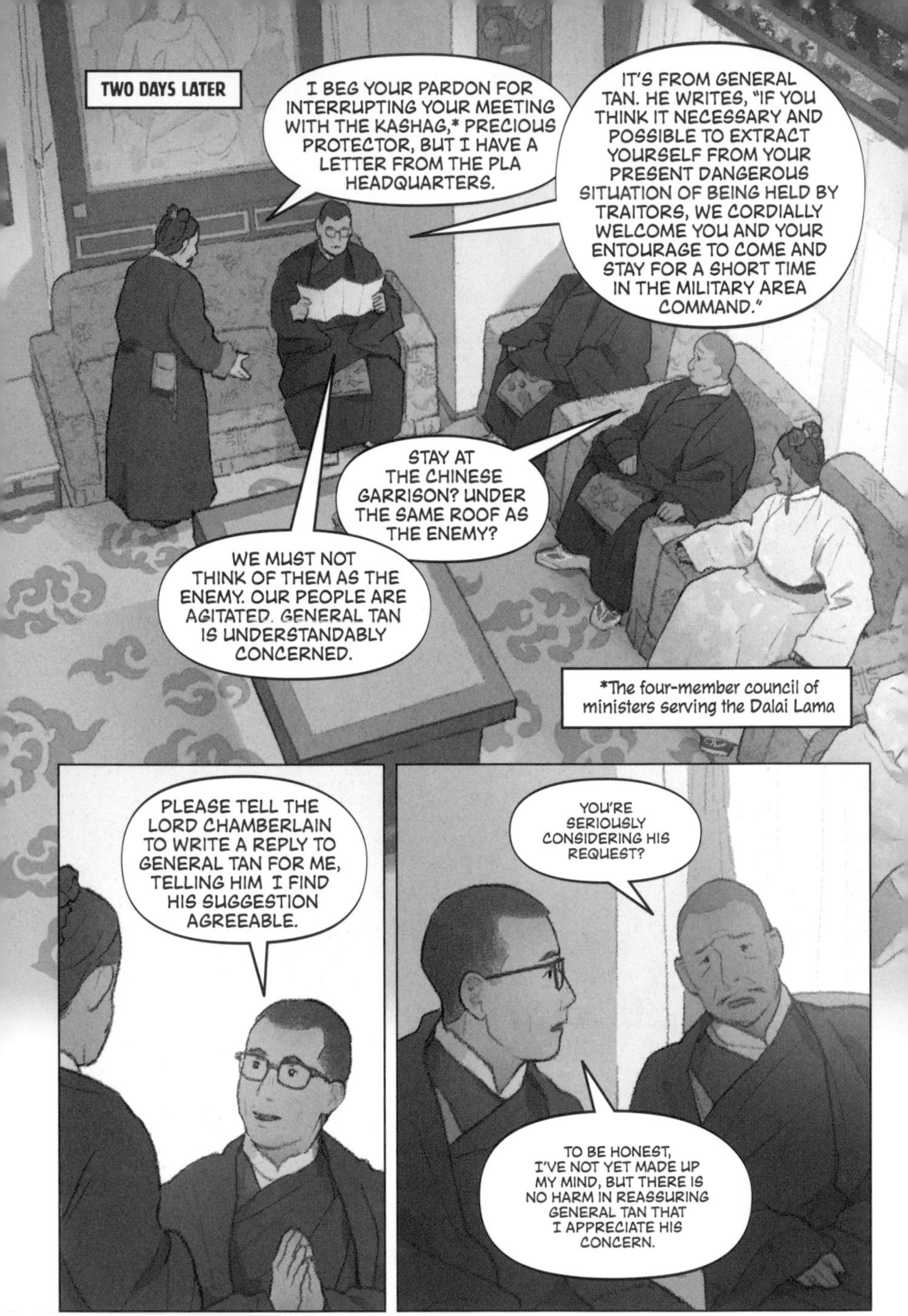
TWO DAYS LATER
I BEG YOUR PARDON FOR INTERRUPTING YOUR MEETING WITH THE KASHAG,* PRECIOUS PROTECTOR, BUT I HAVE A LETTER FROM THE PLA HEADQUARTERS.
IT'S FROM GENERAL TAN. HE WRITES, "IF YOU THINK IT NECESSARY AND POSSIBLE TO EXTRACT YOURSELF FROM YOUR PRESENT DANGEROUS SITUATION OF BEING HELD BY TRAITORS, WE CORDIALLY WELCOME YOU AND YOUR ENTOURAGE TO COME AND STAY FOR A SHORT TIME IN THE MILITARY AREA COMMAND."
STAY AT THE CHINESE GARRISON? UNDER THE SAME ROOF AS THE ENEMY?
WE MUST NOT THINK OF THEM AS THE ENEMY. OUR PEOPLE ARE AGITATED. GENERAL TAN IS UNDERSTANDABLY CONCERNED.
*The four-member council of ministers serving the Dalai Lama
PLEASE TELL THE LORD CHAMBERLAIN TO WRITE A REPLY TO GENERAL TAN FOR ME, TELLING HIM I FIND HIS SUGGESTION AGREEABLE.
YOU'RE SERIOUSLY CONSIDERING HIS REQUEST?
TO BE HONEST, I'VE NOT YET MADE UP MY MIND, BUT THERE IS NO HARM IN REASSURING GENERAL TAN THAT I APPRECIATE HIS CONCERN.

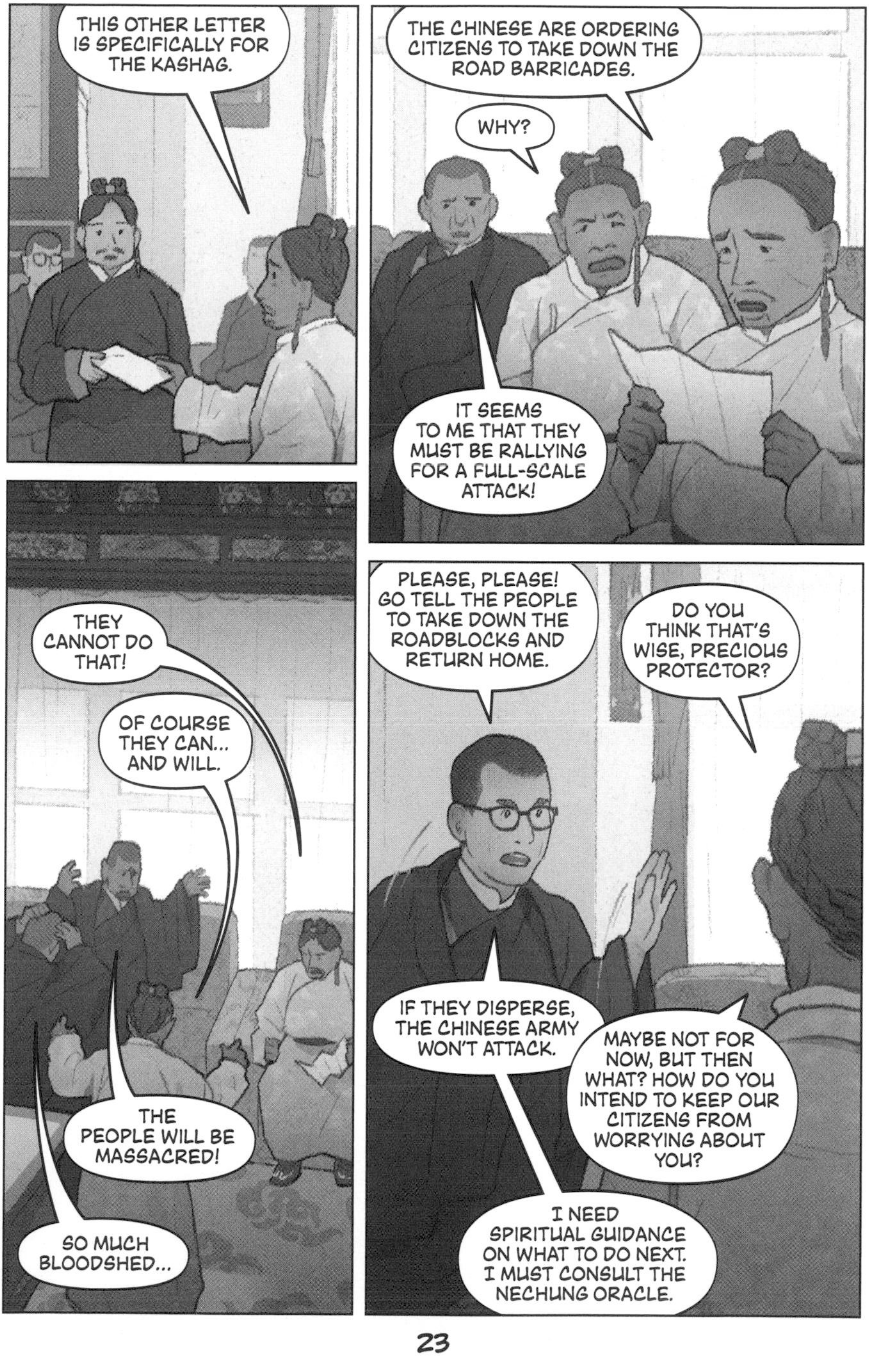
THIS OTHER LETTER IS SPECIFICALLY FOR THE KASHAG.
THE CHINESE ARE ORDERING CITIZENS TO TAKE DOWN THE ROAD BARRICADES.
WHY?
IT SEEMS TO ME THAT THEY MUST BE RALLYING FOR A FULL-SCALE ATTACK!
THEY CANNOT DO THAT!
OF COURSE THEY CAN... AND WILL.
THE PEOPLE WILL BE MASSACRED!
SO MUCH BLOODSHED...
PLEASE, PLEASE! GO TELL THE PEOPLE TO TAKE DOWN THE ROADBLOCKS AND RETURN HOME.
DO YOU THINK THAT'S WISE, PRECIOUS PROTECTOR?
IF THEY DISPERSE, THE CHINESE ARMY WON'T ATTACK.
MAYBE NOT FOR NOW, BUT THEN WHAT? HOW DO YOU INTEND TO KEEP OUR CITIZENS FROM WORRYING ABOUT YOU?
I NEED SPIRITUAL GUIDANCE ON WHAT TO DO NEXT. I MUST CONSULT THE NECHUNG ORACLE.

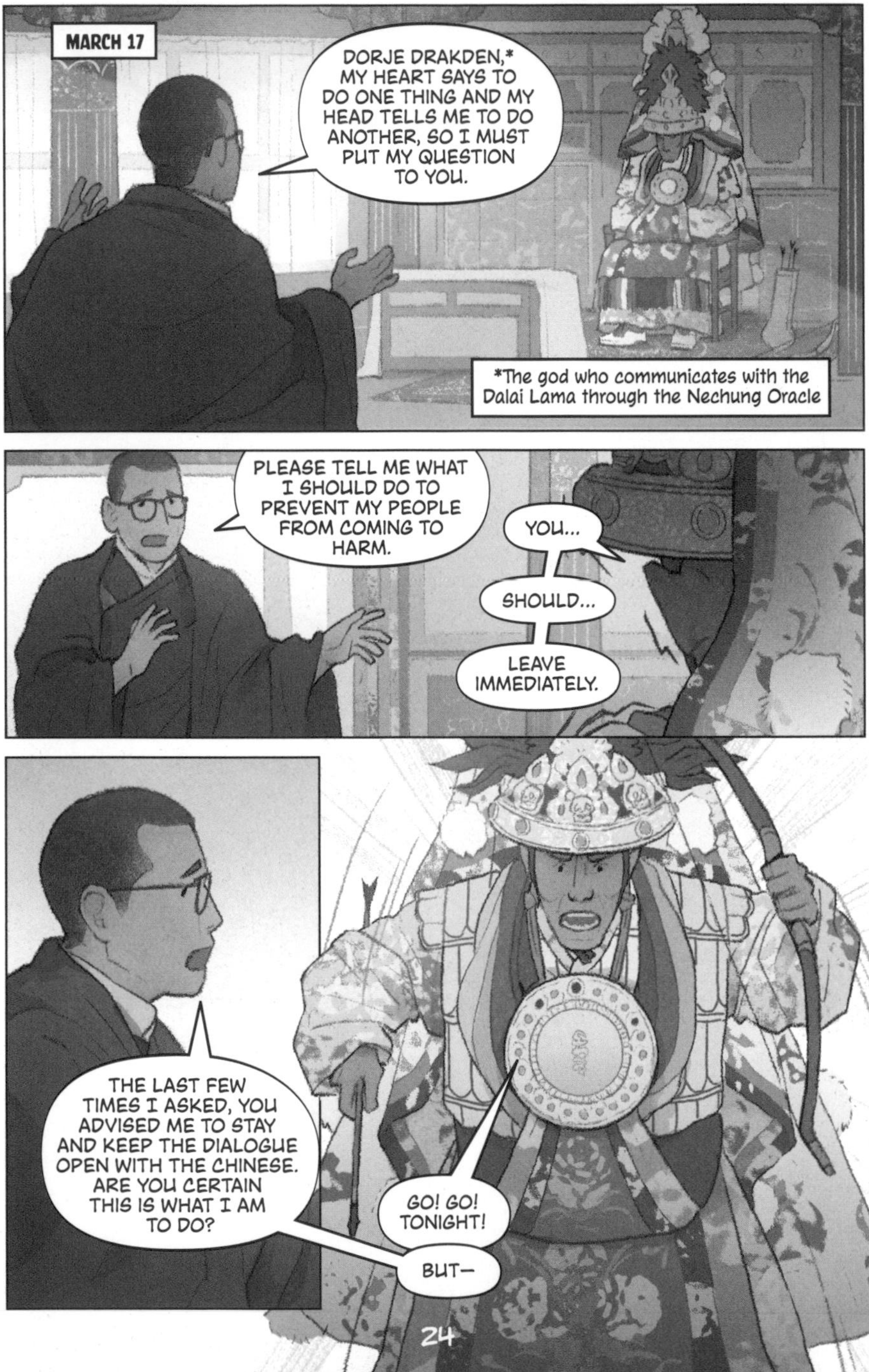
MARCH 17
DORJE DRAKDEN,* MY HEART SAYS TO DO ONE THING AND MY HEAD TELLS ME TO DO ANOTHER, SO I MUST PUT MY QUESTION TO YOU.
*The god who communicates with the Dalai Lama through the Nechung Oracle
PLEASE TELL ME WHAT I SHOULD DO TO PREVENT MY PEOPLE FROM COMING TO HARM.
YOU...
SHOULD...
LEAVE IMMEDIATELY.
THE LAST FEW TIMES I ASKED, YOU ADVISED ME TO STAY AND KEEP THE DIALOGUE OPEN WITH THE CHINESE. ARE YOU CERTAIN THIS IS WHAT I AM TO DO?
GO! GO! TONIGHT!
BUT—

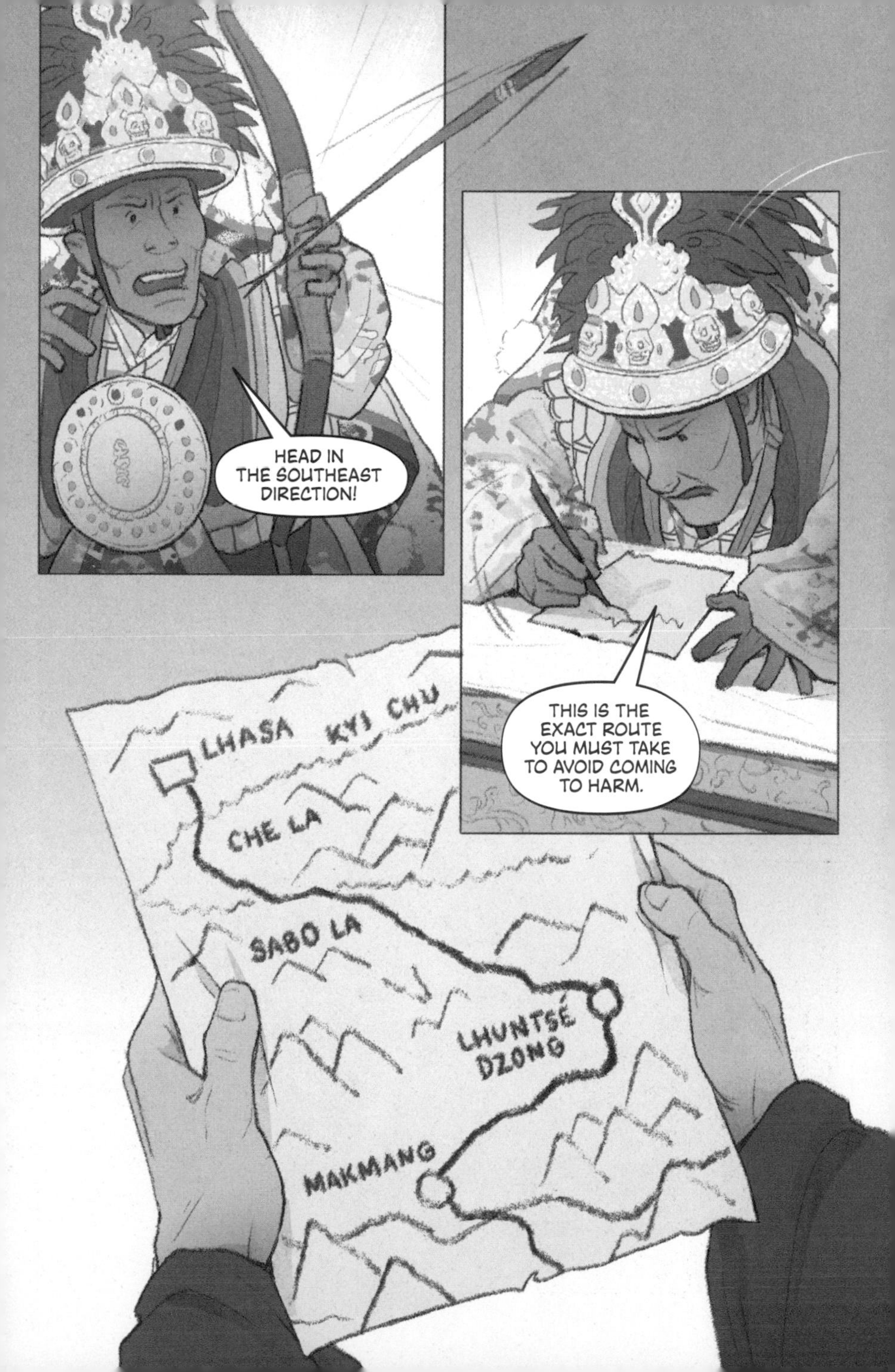
HEAD IN THE SOUTHEAST DIRECTION!
THIS IS THE EXACT ROUTE YOU MUST TAKE TO AVOID COMING TO HARM.
LHASA
KYI CHU
CHE LA
SABO LA
LHUNTSÉ DZONG
MAKMANG

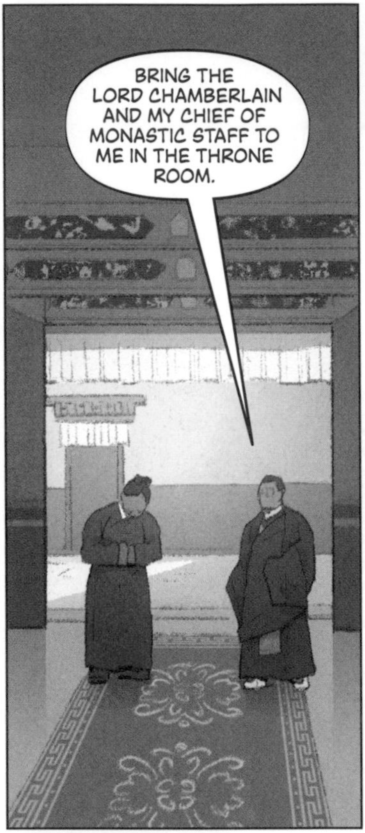
BRING THE LORD CHAMBERLAIN AND MY CHIEF OF MONASTIC STAFF TO ME IN THE THRONE ROOM.

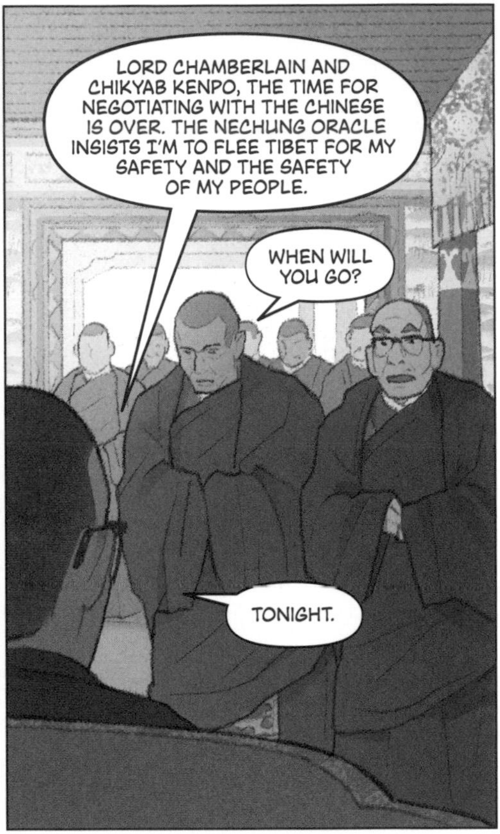
LORD CHAMBERLAIN AND CHIKYAB KENPO, THE TIME FOR NEGOTIATING WITH THE CHINESE IS OVER. THE NECHUNG ORACLE INSISTS I'M TO FLEE TIBET FOR MY SAFETY AND THE SAFETY OF MY PEOPLE.
WHEN WILL YOU GO?
TONIGHT.

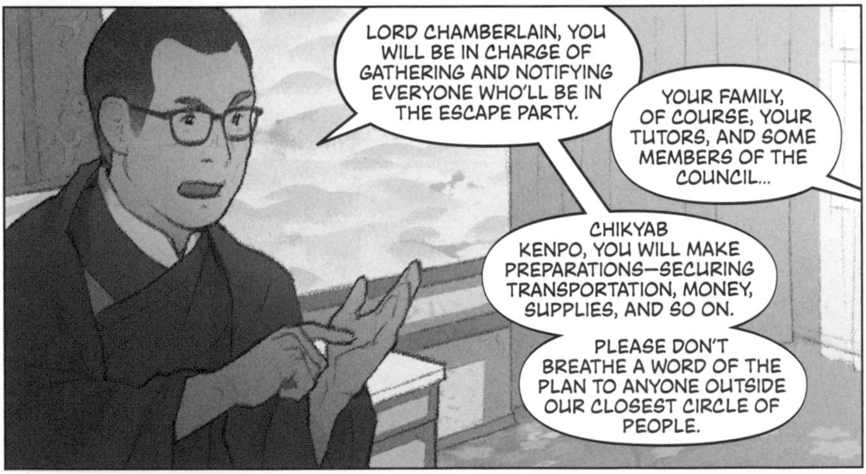
LORD CHAMBERLAIN, YOU WILL BE IN CHARGE OF GATHERING AND NOTIFYING EVERYONE WHO'LL BE IN THE ESCAPE PARTY.
YOUR FAMILY, OF COURSE, YOUR TUTORS, AND SOME MEMBERS OF THE COUNCIL...
CHIKYAB KENPO, YOU WILL MAKE PREPARATIONS—SECURING TRANSPORTATION, MONEY, SUPPLIES, AND SO ON.
PLEASE DON'T BREATHE A WORD OF THE PLAN TO ANYONE OUTSIDE OUR CLOSEST CIRCLE OF PEOPLE.

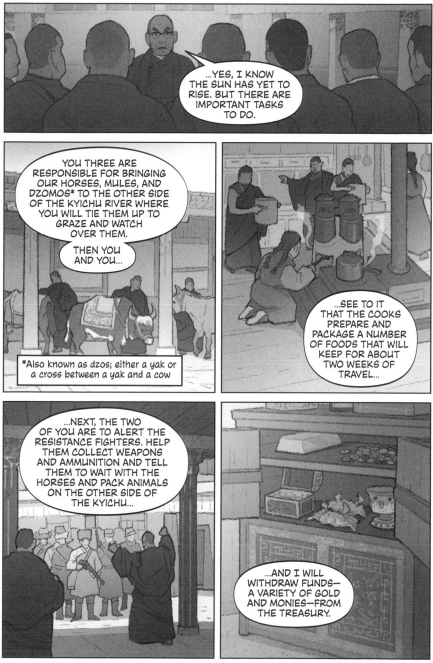

...YES, I KNOW THE SUN HAS YET TO RISE. BUT THERE ARE IMPORTANT TASKS TO DO.

YOU THREE ARE RESPONSIBLE FOR BRINGING OUR HORSES, MULES, AND DZOMOS* TO THE OTHER SIDE OF THE KYICHU RIVER WHERE YOU WILL TIE THEM UP TO GRAZE AND WATCH OVER THEM.

THEN YOU AND YOU...

*Also known as dzos; either a yak or a cross between a yak and a cow

...SEE TO IT THAT THE COOKS PREPARE AND PACKAGE A NUMBER OF FOODS THAT WILL KEEP FOR ABOUT TWO WEEKS OF TRAVEL...

...NEXT, THE TWO OF YOU ARE TO ALERT THE RESISTANCE FIGHTERS. HELP THEM COLLECT WEAPONS AND AMMUNITION AND TELL THEM TO WAIT WITH THE HORSES AND PACK ANIMALS ON THE OTHER SIDE OF THE KYICHU...

...AND I WILL WITHDRAW FUNDS— A VARIETY OF GOLD AND MONIES—FROM THE TREASURY.

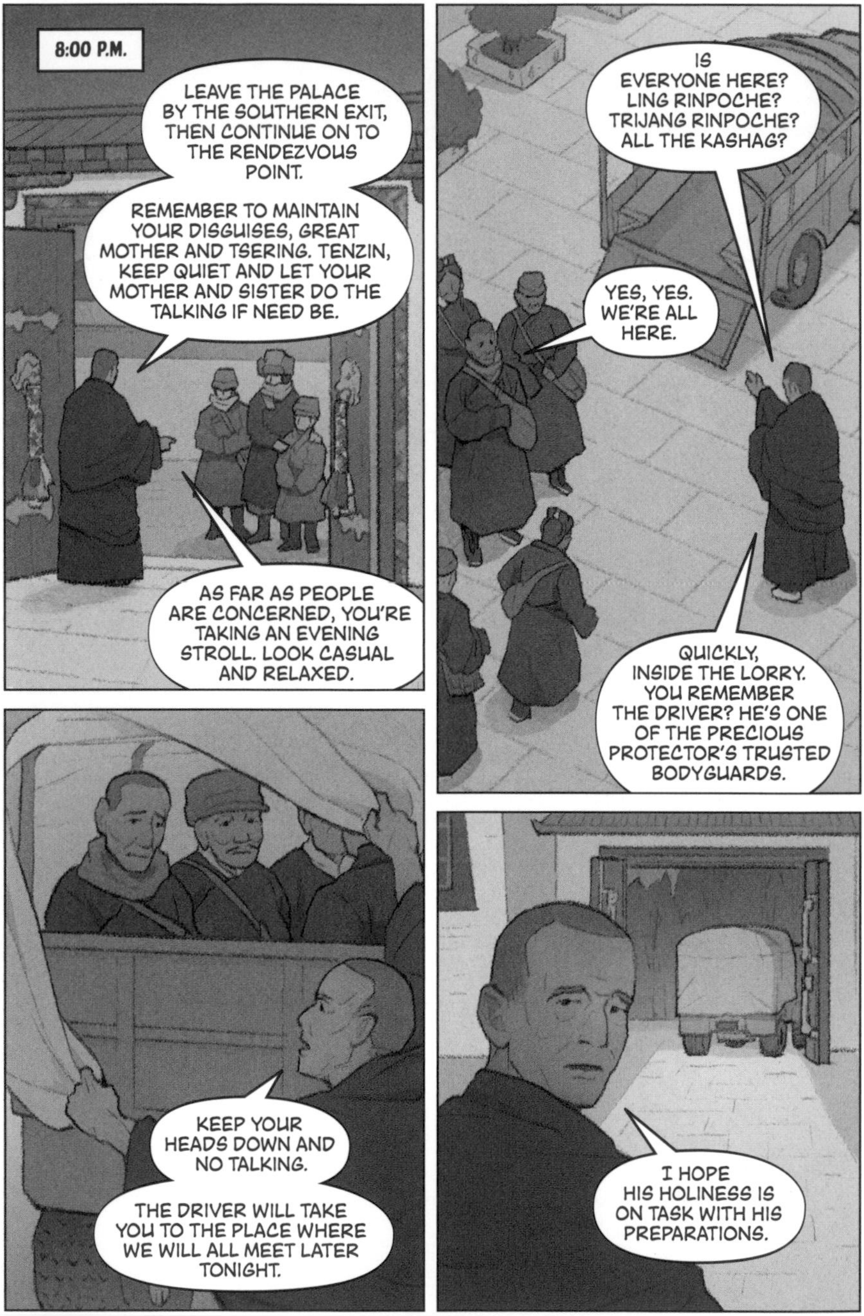
8:00 P.M.
LEAVE THE PALACE BY THE SOUTHERN EXIT, THEN CONTINUE ON TO THE RENDEZVOUS POINT.
REMEMBER TO MAINTAIN YOUR DISGUISES, GREAT MOTHER AND TSERING. TENZIN, KEEP QUIET AND LET YOUR MOTHER AND SISTER DO THE TALKING IF NEED BE.
AS FAR AS PEOPLE ARE CONCERNED, YOU'RE TAKING AN EVENING STROLL. LOOK CASUAL AND RELAXED.
IS EVERYONE HERE? LING RINPOCHE? TRIJANG RINPOCHE? ALL THE KASHAG?
YES, YES. WE'RE ALL HERE.
QUICKLY, INSIDE THE LORRY. YOU REMEMBER THE DRIVER? HE'S ONE OF THE PRECIOUS PROTECTOR'S TRUSTED BODYGUARDS.
KEEP YOUR HEADS DOWN AND NO TALKING.
THE DRIVER WILL TAKE YOU TO THE PLACE WHERE WE WILL ALL MEET LATER TONIGHT.
I HOPE HIS HOLINESS IS ON TASK WITH HIS PREPARATIONS.

Lord Chamberlain

Even though the Dalai Lama is known as "Precious Protector," Tibetans also try to keep *him* under protection. Not only do they want to shield him from any physical danger, because they also consider him the living embodiment of Buddha, and therefore a god, they also want to spare him the daily grind and toil that ordinary humans endure.

To do that, Tibetans created a court of personal attendants consisting of upper status monks. And the head of this court, in the highest-ranking position below the Dalai Lama, is the Lord Chamberlain (otherwise known as Phala). Three clerical aides (the Kenpos) help the Lord Chamberlain supervise the personal attendants in ensuring that the Dalai Lama's needs with respect to food, daily living, and religious ceremony are met.

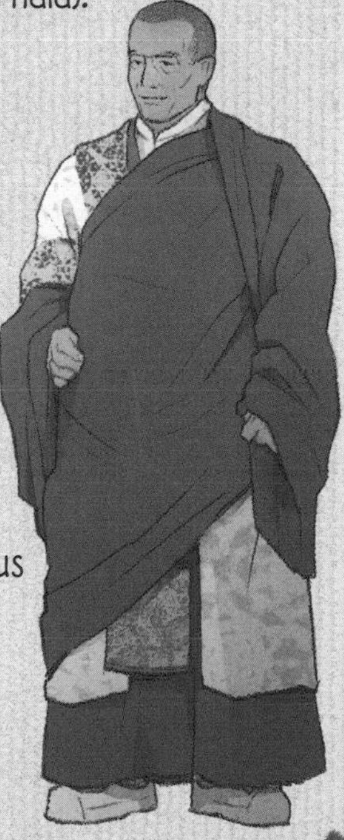

Phala Thupten Woden served as the 14th Dalai Lama's Lord Chamberlain during the period covered in this book. Having accompanied the Precious Protector on his escape from Lhasa, Lord Chamberlain never got to see his homeland again. He died in 1985.

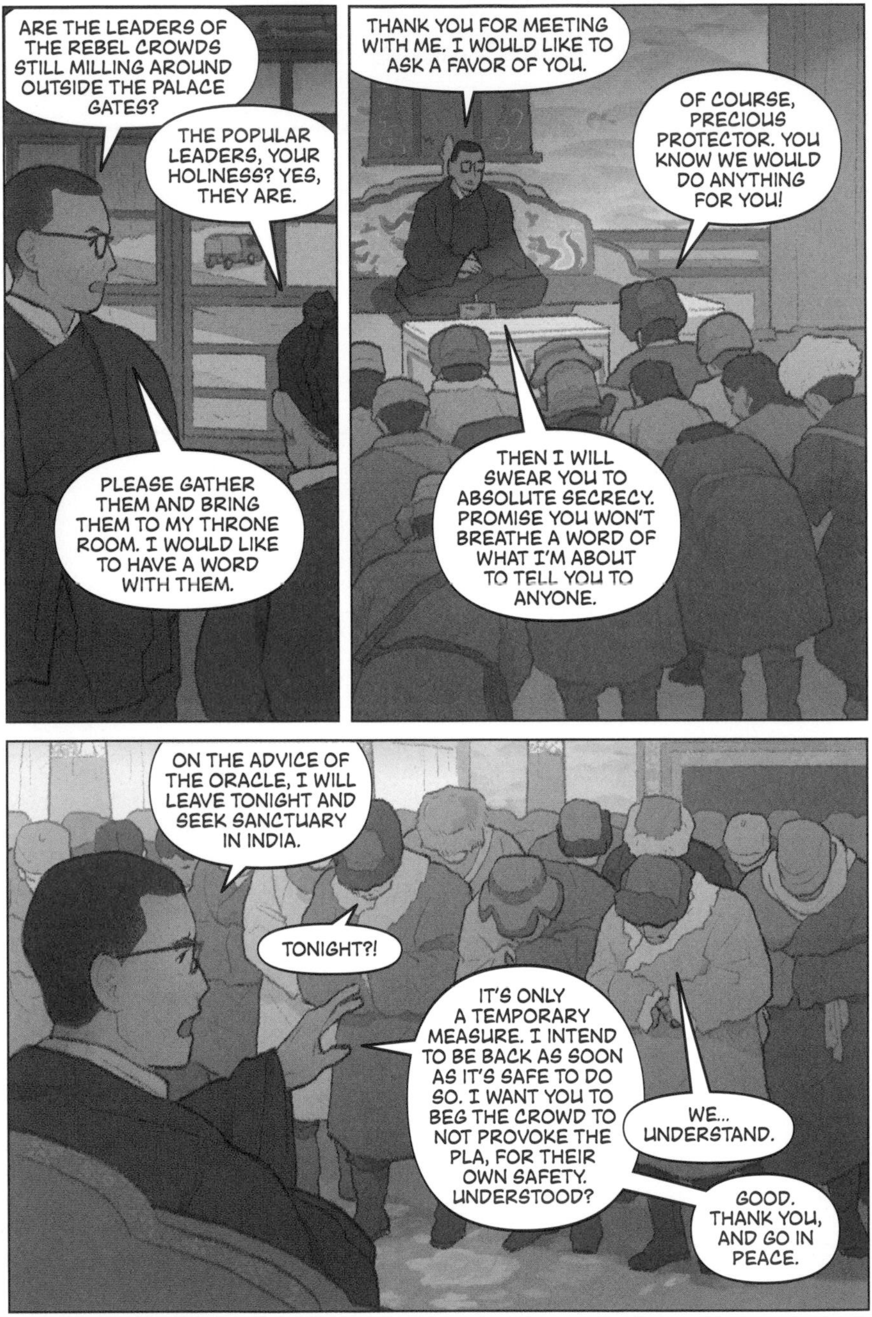
ARE THE LEADERS OF THE REBEL CROWDS STILL MILLING AROUND OUTSIDE THE PALACE GATES?
THE POPULAR LEADERS, YOUR HOLINESS? YES, THEY ARE.
PLEASE GATHER THEM AND BRING THEM TO MY THRONE ROOM. I WOULD LIKE TO HAVE A WORD WITH THEM.
THANK YOU FOR MEETING WITH ME. I WOULD LIKE TO ASK A FAVOR OF YOU.
OF COURSE, PRECIOUS PROTECTOR. YOU KNOW WE WOULD DO ANYTHING FOR YOU!
THEN I WILL SWEAR YOU TO ABSOLUTE SECRECY. PROMISE YOU WON'T BREATHE A WORD OF WHAT I'M ABOUT TO TELL YOU TO ANYONE.
ON THE ADVICE OF THE ORACLE, I WILL LEAVE TONIGHT AND SEEK SANCTUARY IN INDIA.
TONIGHT?!
IT'S ONLY A TEMPORARY MEASURE. I INTEND TO BE BACK AS SOON AS IT'S SAFE TO DO SO. I WANT YOU TO BEG THE CROWD TO NOT PROVOKE THE PLA, FOR THEIR OWN SAFETY. UNDERSTOOD?
WE... UNDERSTAND.
GOOD. THANK YOU, AND GO IN PEACE.

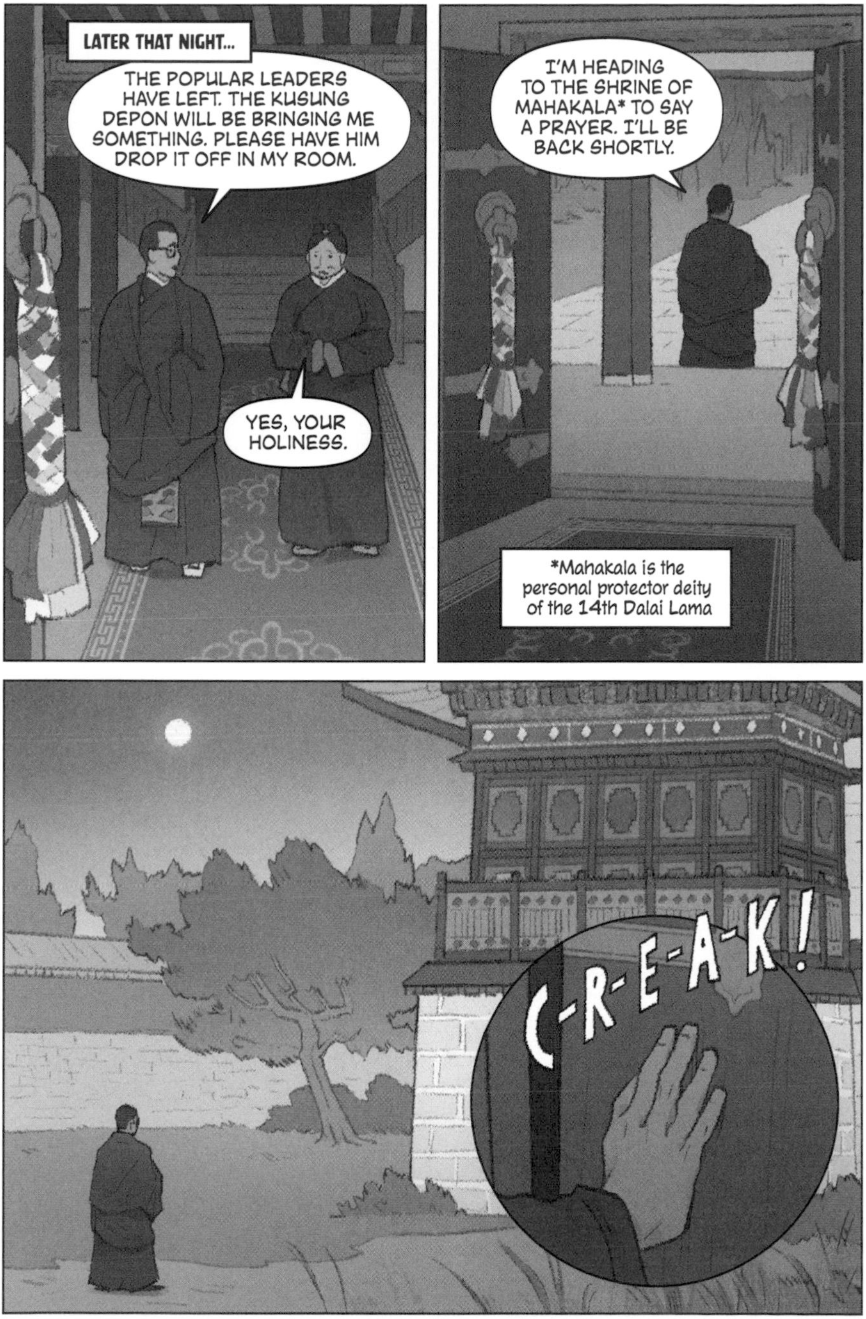
LATER THAT NIGHT...
THE POPULAR LEADERS HAVE LEFT. THE KUSUNG DEPON WILL BE BRINGING ME SOMETHING. PLEASE HAVE HIM DROP IT OFF IN MY ROOM.
YES, YOUR HOLINESS.
I'M HEADING TO THE SHRINE OF MAHAKALA* TO SAY A PRAYER. I'LL BE BACK SHORTLY.
*Mahakala is the personal protector deity of the 14th Dalai Lama
C-R-E-A-K!

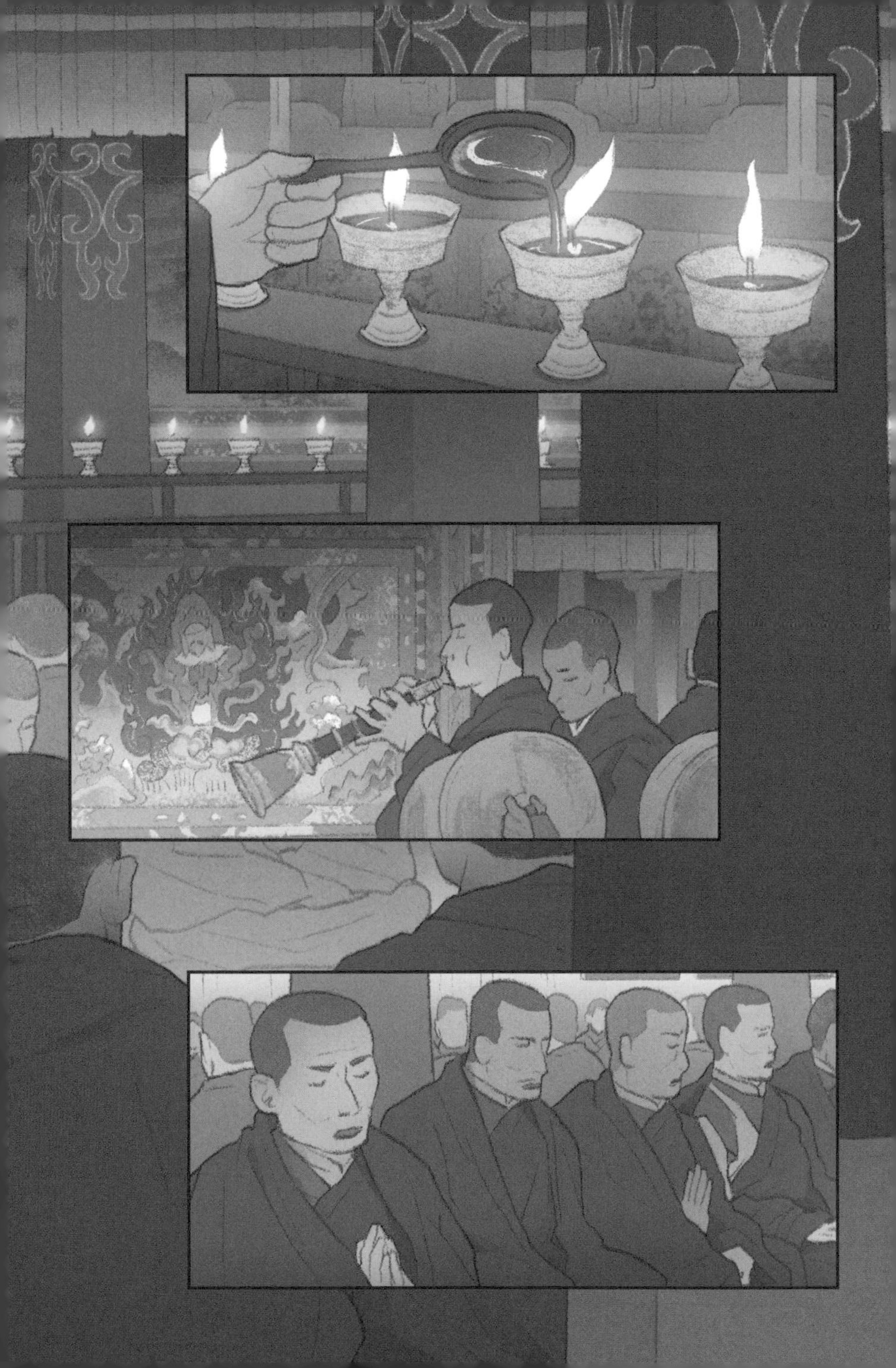

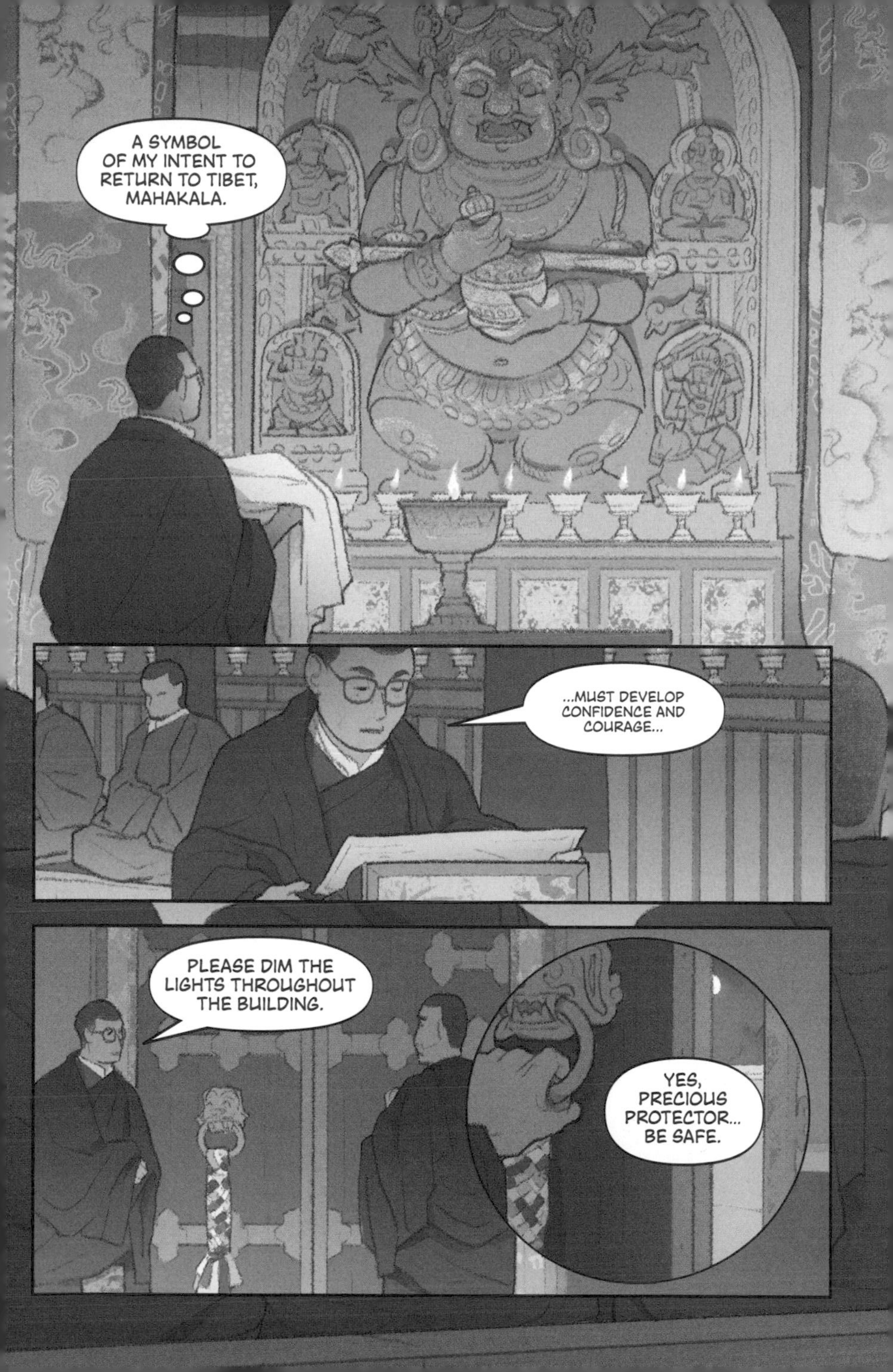
A SYMBOL OF MY INTENT TO RETURN TO TIBET, MAHAKALA.
...MUST DEVELOP CONFIDENCE AND COURAGE...
PLEASE DIM THE LIGHTS THROUGHOUT THE BUILDING.
YES, PRECIOUS PROTECTOR... BE SAFE.

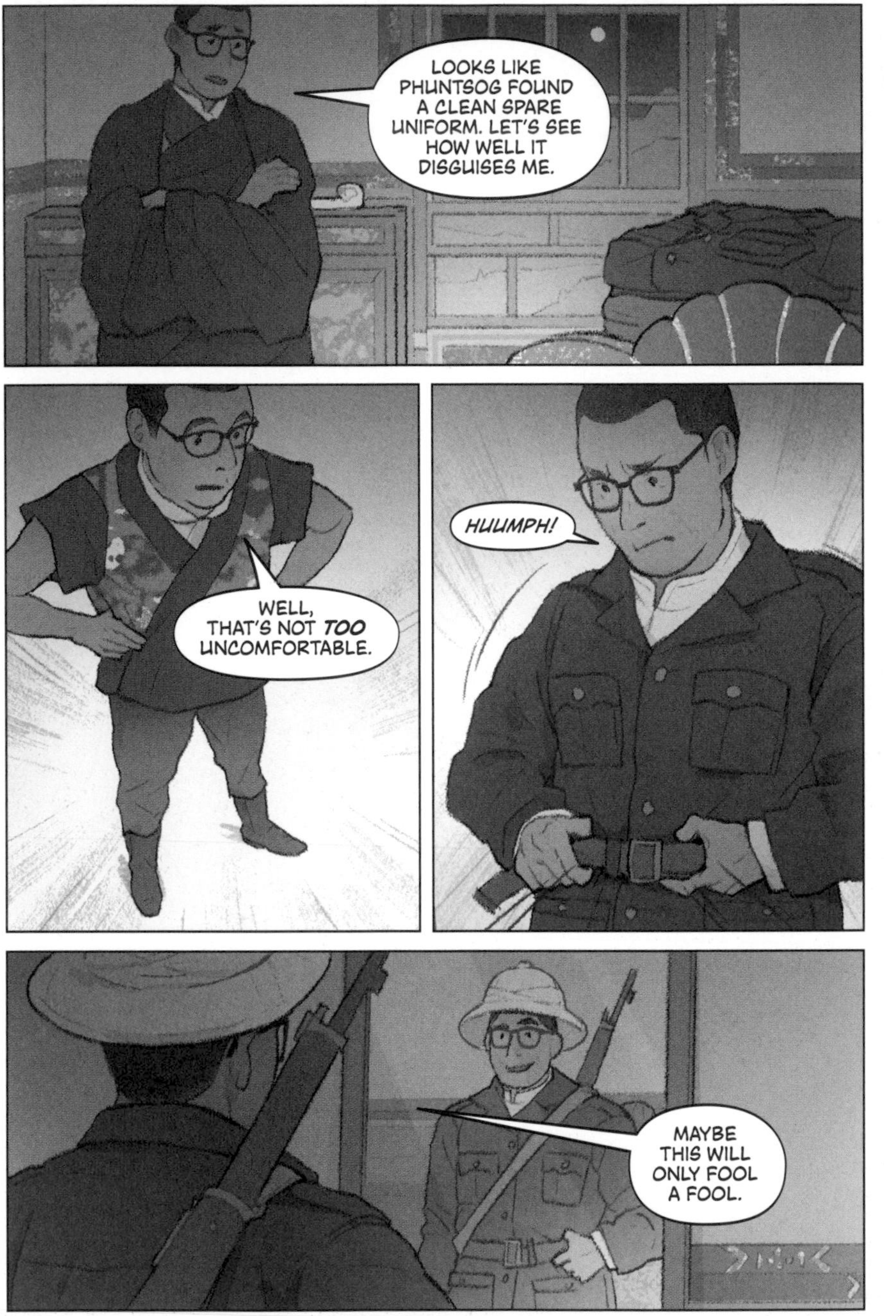
LOOKS LIKE PHUNTSOG FOUND A CLEAN SPARE UNIFORM. LET'S SEE HOW WELL IT DISGUISES ME.
WELL, THAT'S NOT *TOO* UNCOMFORTABLE.
HUUMPH!
MAYBE THIS WILL ONLY FOOL A FOOL.

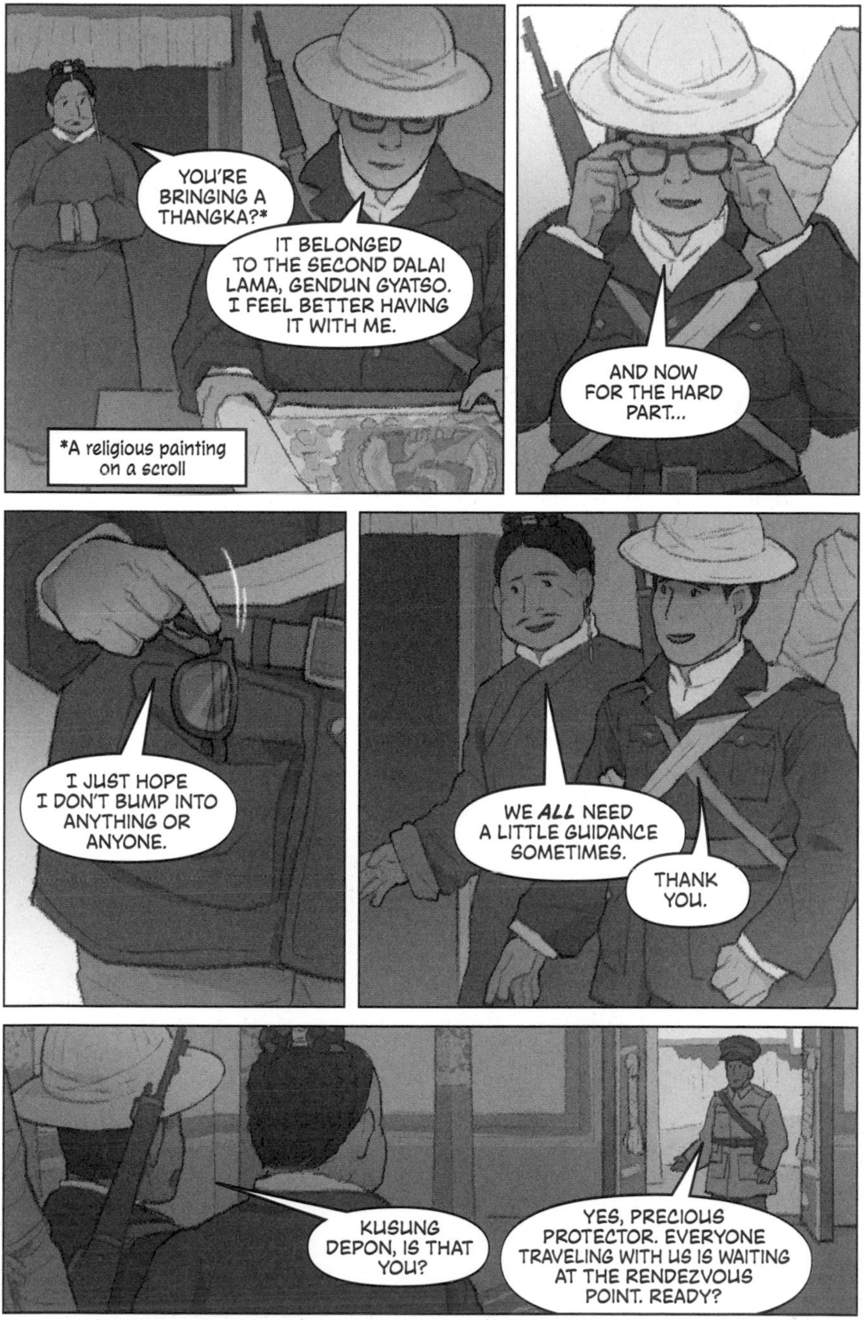

YOU'RE BRINGING A THANGKA?*
IT BELONGED TO THE SECOND DALAI LAMA, GENDUN GYATSO. I FEEL BETTER HAVING IT WITH ME.
*A religious painting on a scroll
AND NOW FOR THE HARD PART...
I JUST HOPE I DON'T BUMP INTO ANYTHING OR ANYONE.
WE *ALL* NEED A LITTLE GUIDANCE SOMETIMES.
THANK YOU.
KUSUNG DEPON, IS THAT YOU?
YES, PRECIOUS PROTECTOR. EVERYONE TRAVELING WITH US IS WAITING AT THE RENDEZVOUS POINT. READY?

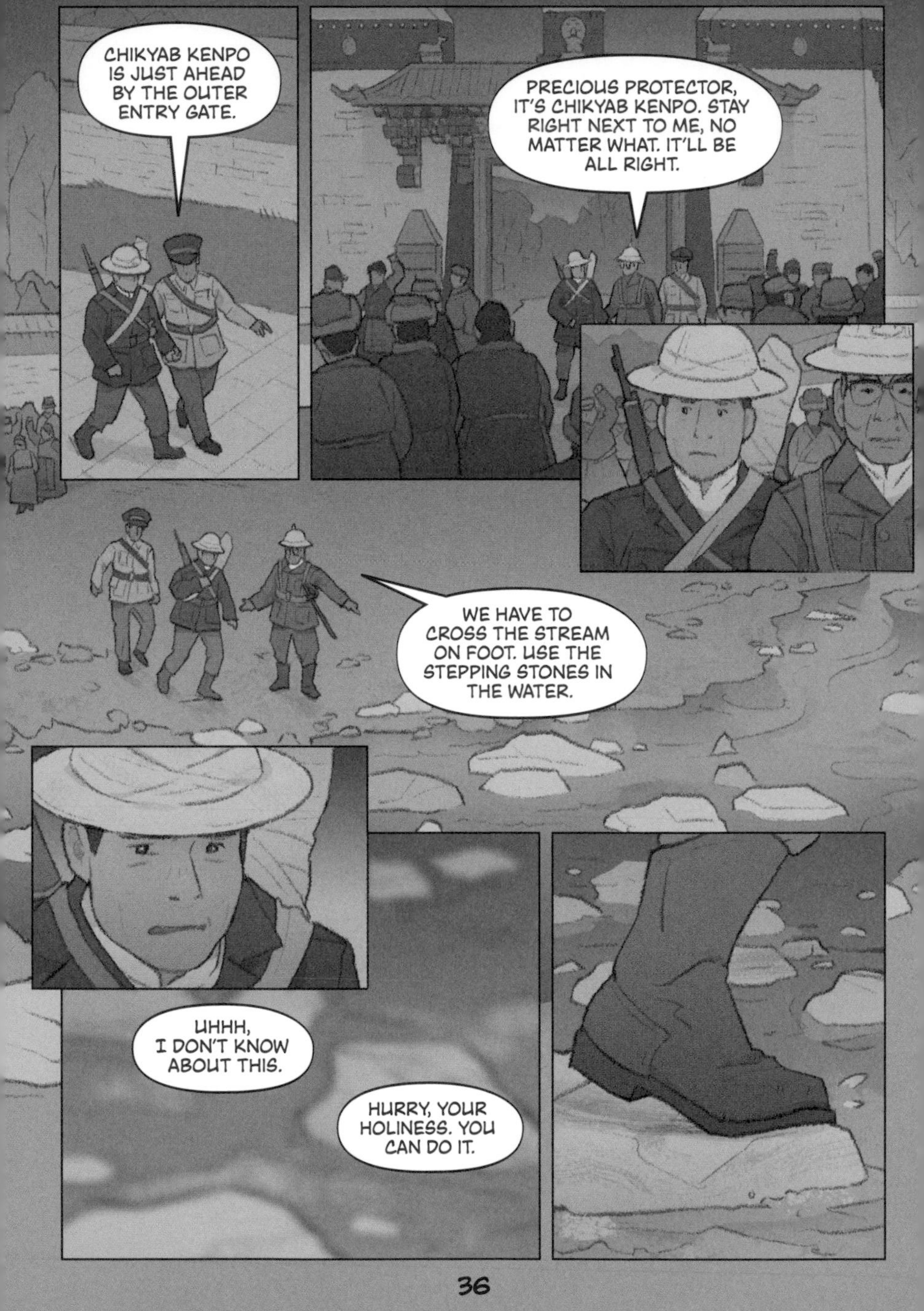
CHIKYAB KENPO IS JUST AHEAD BY THE OUTER ENTRY GATE.
PRECIOUS PROTECTOR, IT'S CHIKYAB KENPO. STAY RIGHT NEXT TO ME, NO MATTER WHAT. IT'LL BE ALL RIGHT.
WE HAVE TO CROSS THE STREAM ON FOOT. USE THE STEPPING STONES IN THE WATER.
UHHH, I DON'T KNOW ABOUT THIS.
HURRY, YOUR HOLINESS. YOU CAN DO IT.

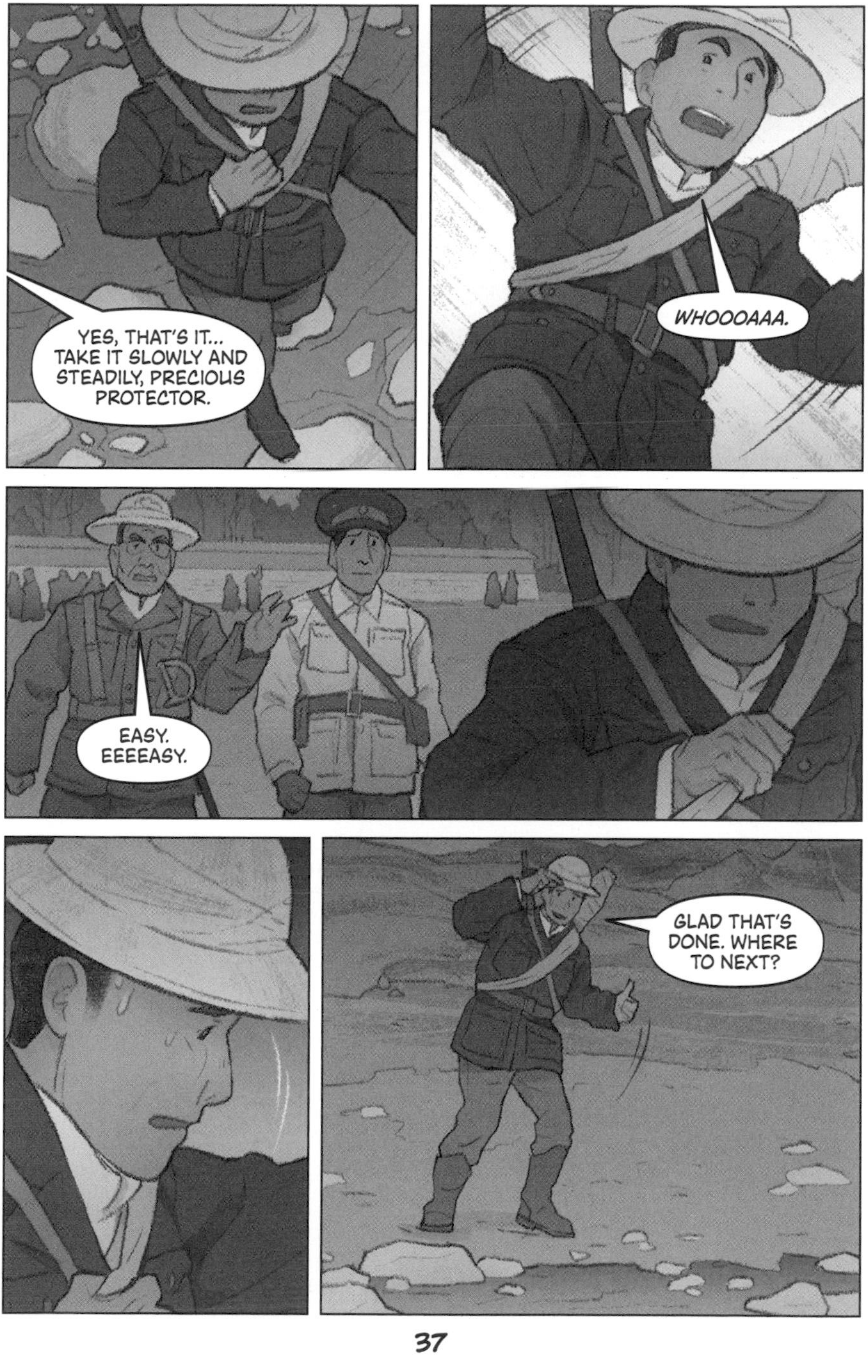
YES, THAT'S IT... TAKE IT SLOWLY AND STEADILY, PRECIOUS PROTECTOR.
WHOOOAAA.
EASY. EEEEASY.
GLAD THAT'S DONE. WHERE TO NEXT?

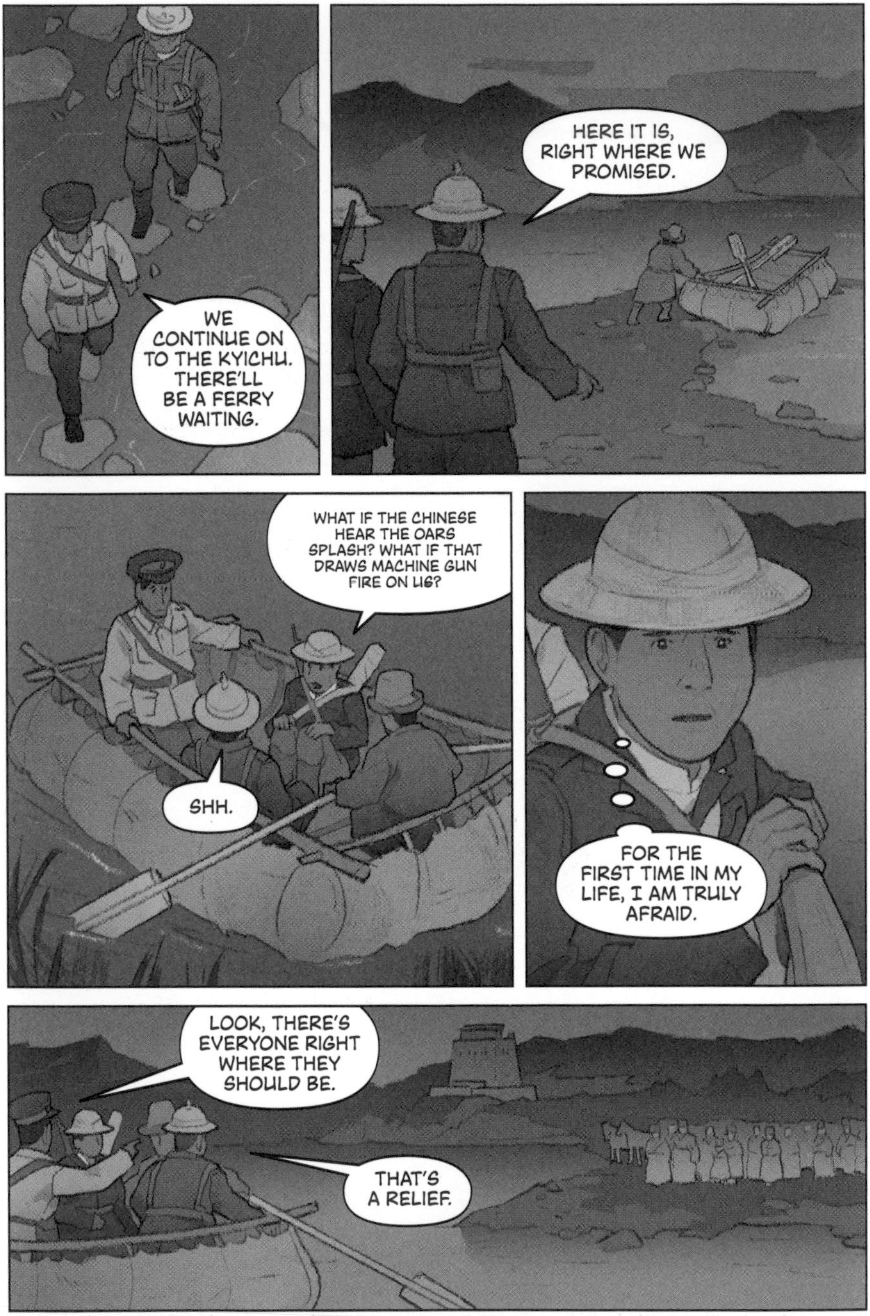
WE CONTINUE ON TO THE KYICHU. THERE'LL BE A FERRY WAITING.
HERE IT IS, RIGHT WHERE WE PROMISED.
WHAT IF THE CHINESE HEAR THE OARS SPLASH? WHAT IF THAT DRAWS MACHINE GUN FIRE ON US?
SHH.
FOR THE FIRST TIME IN MY LIFE, I AM TRULY AFRAID.
LOOK, THERE'S EVERYONE RIGHT WHERE THEY SHOULD BE.
THAT'S A RELIEF.

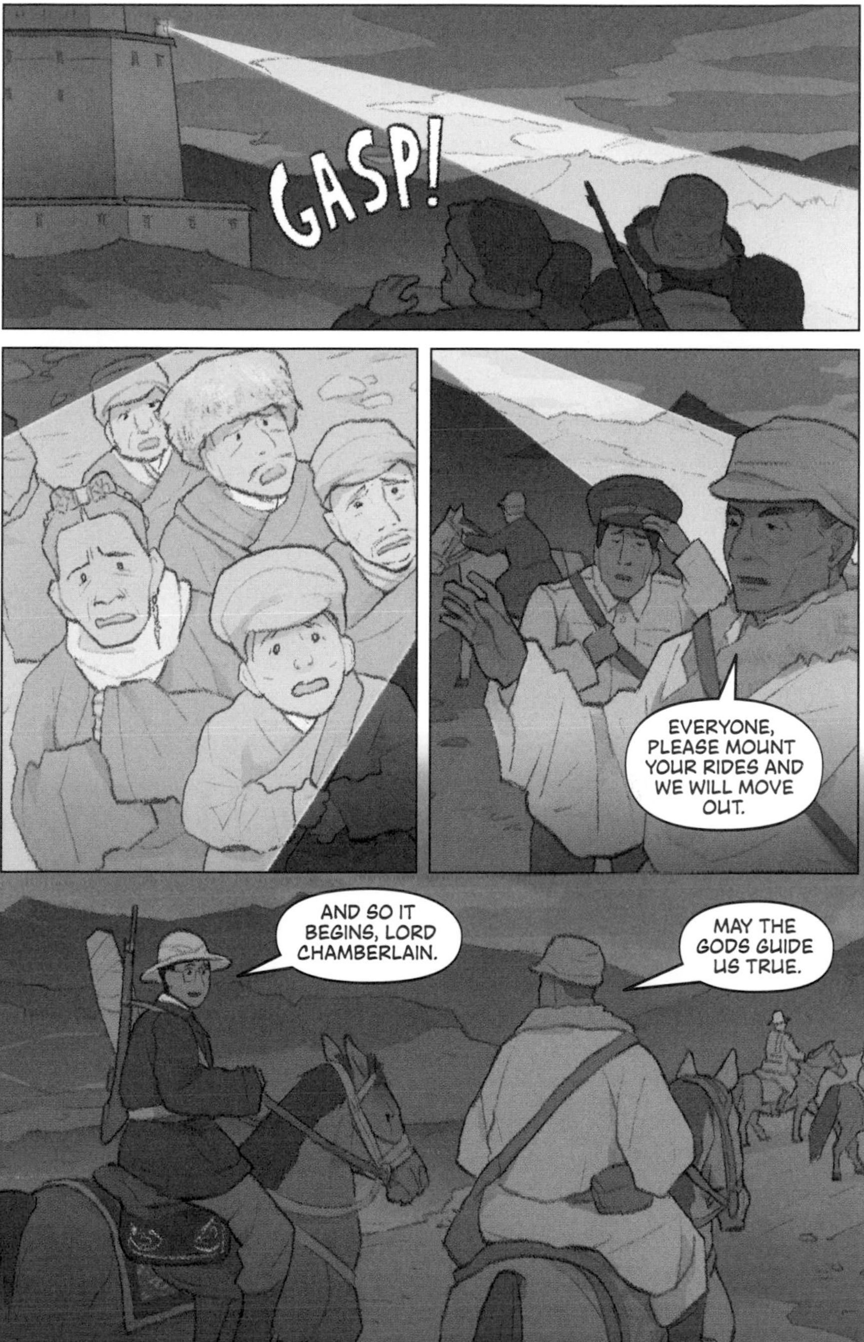
GASP!
EVERYONE, PLEASE MOUNT YOUR RIDES AND WE WILL MOVE OUT.
AND SO IT BEGINS, LORD CHAMBERLAIN.
MAY THE GODS GUIDE US TRUE.

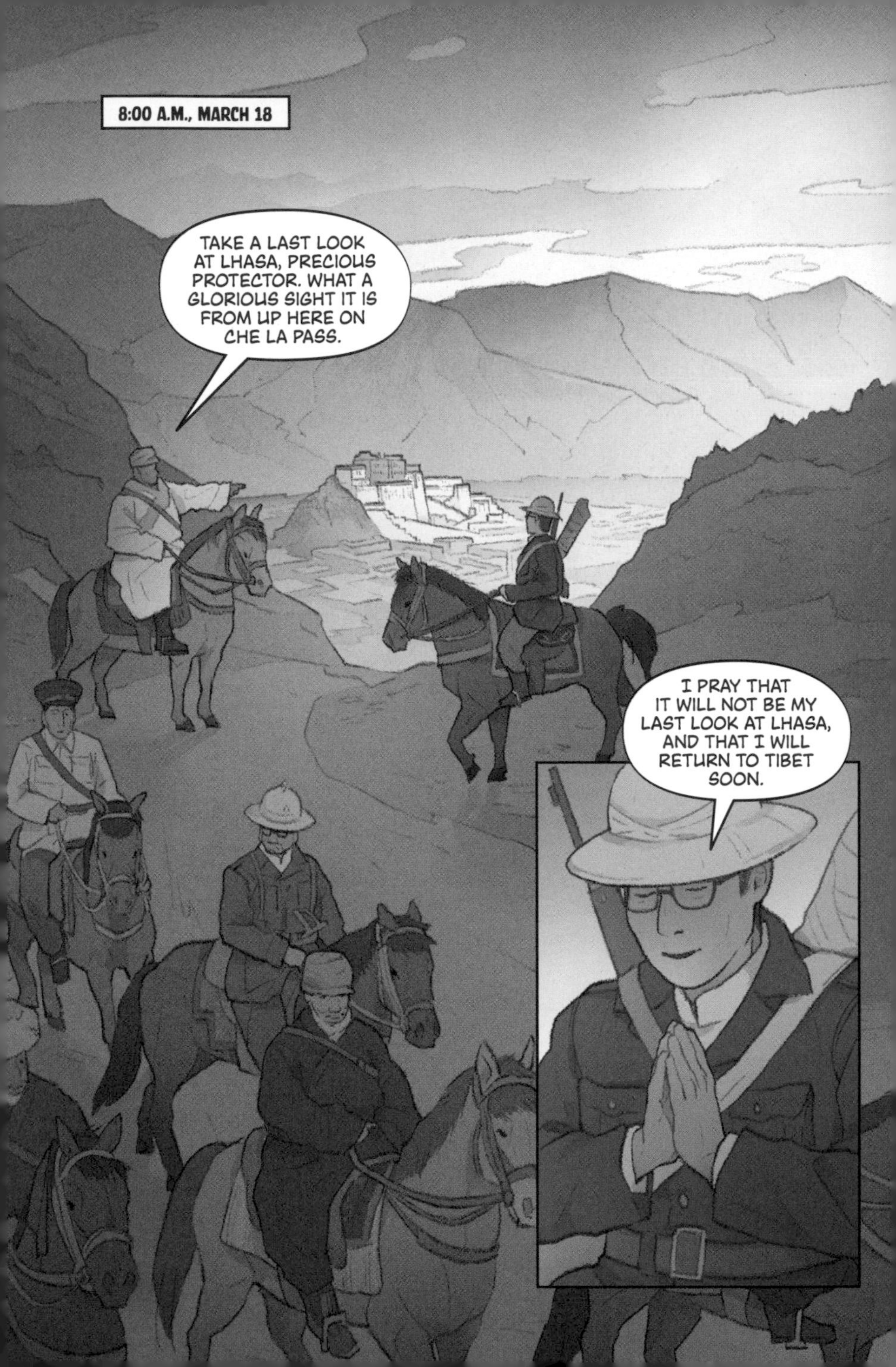
8:00 A.M., MARCH 18
TAKE A LAST LOOK AT LHASA, PRECIOUS PROTECTOR. WHAT A GLORIOUS SIGHT IT IS FROM UP HERE ON CHE LA PASS.
I PRAY THAT IT WILL NOT BE MY LAST LOOK AT LHASA, AND THAT I WILL RETURN TO TIBET SOON.

Tibet བོད།
The Land of the Snow Lion

Located at the center of East, South, and Inner Asia, Tibet has the greatest elevation of any country on earth, with Mount Everest being its (and the world's) highest peak. While people have lived in the Tibetan Plateau since at least twenty-one thousand years ago, Tibet as an empire, or country, didn't form until the seventh century. Since then, it's been the ancestral homeland to the Tibetan people along with other ethnic groups such as the Monpa, Tamang, Qiang, Sherpa, and Lhoba.

Many people of Tibet are subsistence farmers and herders, meaning they grow food to feed only their own families, and not to sell or export. Tibetans have also adopted the majestic, mythical Snow Lion as their emblem. This creature not only represents the snowy mountain peaks surrounding the country, but also symbolizes strength, power, fearlessness, and joy.

Throughout the centuries, Tibet and China have gone through many diplomatic eras, some friendly and some warring. Unfortunately for the 14th Dalai Lama, it is during the troubled, warring times that he has had to rule.

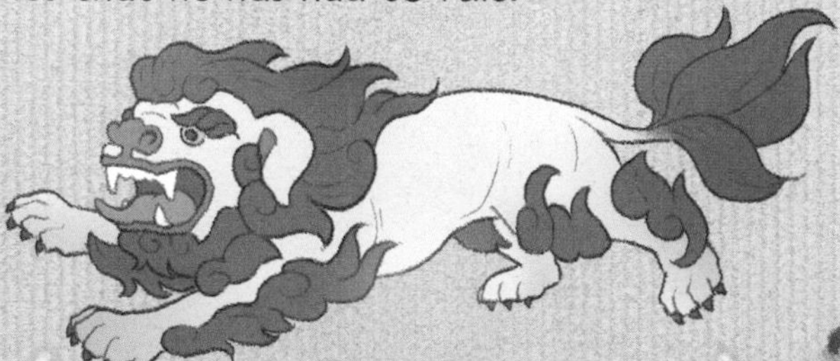

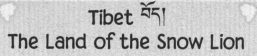

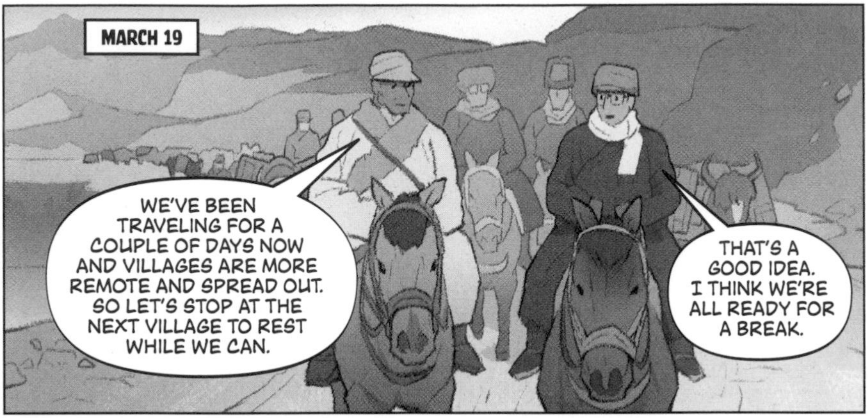
MARCH 19
WE'VE BEEN TRAVELING FOR A COUPLE OF DAYS NOW AND VILLAGES ARE MORE REMOTE AND SPREAD OUT. SO LET'S STOP AT THE NEXT VILLAGE TO REST WHILE WE CAN.
THAT'S A GOOD IDEA. I THINK WE'RE ALL READY FOR A BREAK.

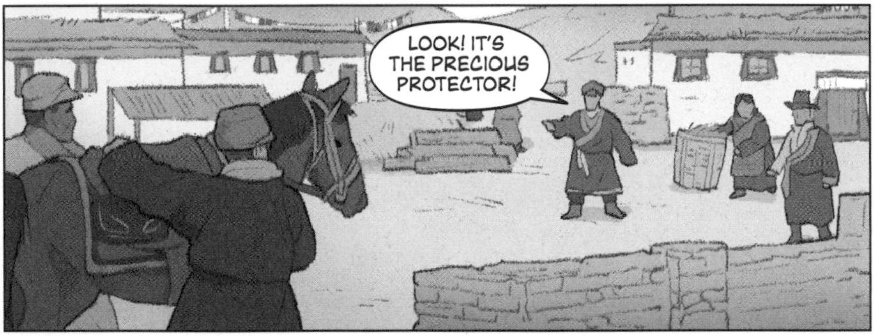
LOOK! IT'S THE PRECIOUS PROTECTOR!

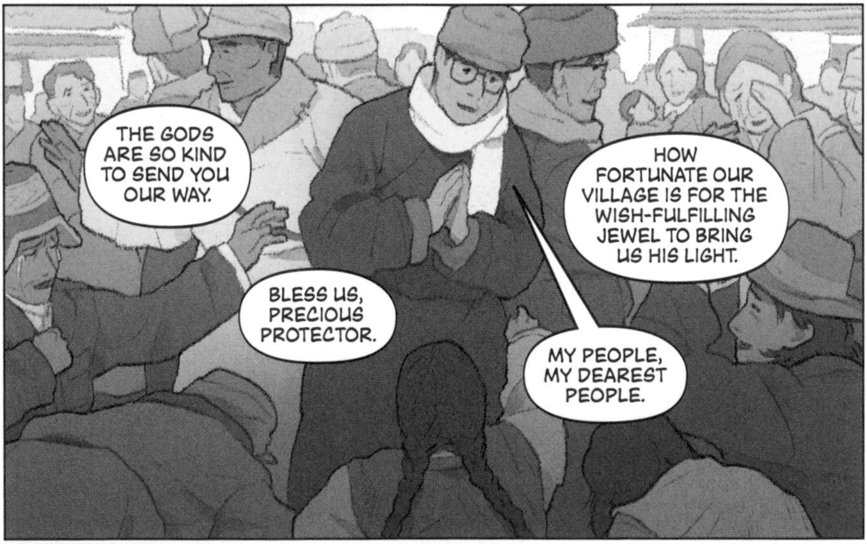
THE GODS ARE SO KIND TO SEND YOU OUR WAY.
HOW FORTUNATE OUR VILLAGE IS FOR THE WISH-FULFILLING JEWEL TO BRING US HIS LIGHT.
BLESS US, PRECIOUS PROTECTOR.
MY PEOPLE, MY DEAREST PEOPLE.

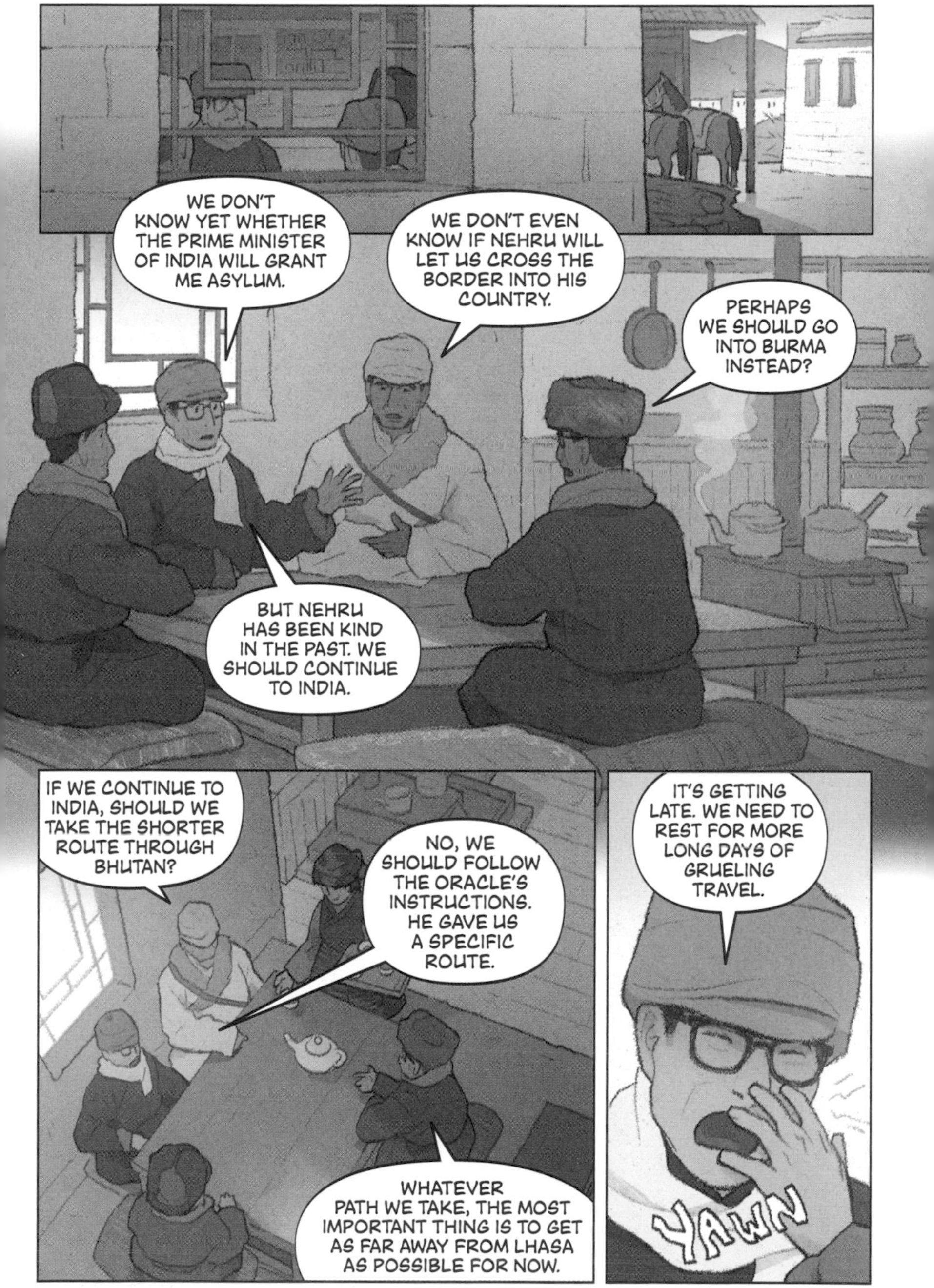
WE DON'T KNOW YET WHETHER THE PRIME MINISTER OF INDIA WILL GRANT ME ASYLUM.
WE DON'T EVEN KNOW IF NEHRU WILL LET US CROSS THE BORDER INTO HIS COUNTRY.
PERHAPS WE SHOULD GO INTO BURMA INSTEAD?
BUT NEHRU HAS BEEN KIND IN THE PAST. WE SHOULD CONTINUE TO INDIA.
IF WE CONTINUE TO INDIA, SHOULD WE TAKE THE SHORTER ROUTE THROUGH BHUTAN?
NO, WE SHOULD FOLLOW THE ORACLE'S INSTRUCTIONS. HE GAVE US A SPECIFIC ROUTE.
WHATEVER PATH WE TAKE, THE MOST IMPORTANT THING IS TO GET AS FAR AWAY FROM LHASA AS POSSIBLE FOR NOW.
IT'S GETTING LATE. WE NEED TO REST FOR MORE LONG DAYS OF GRUELING TRAVEL.
YAWN

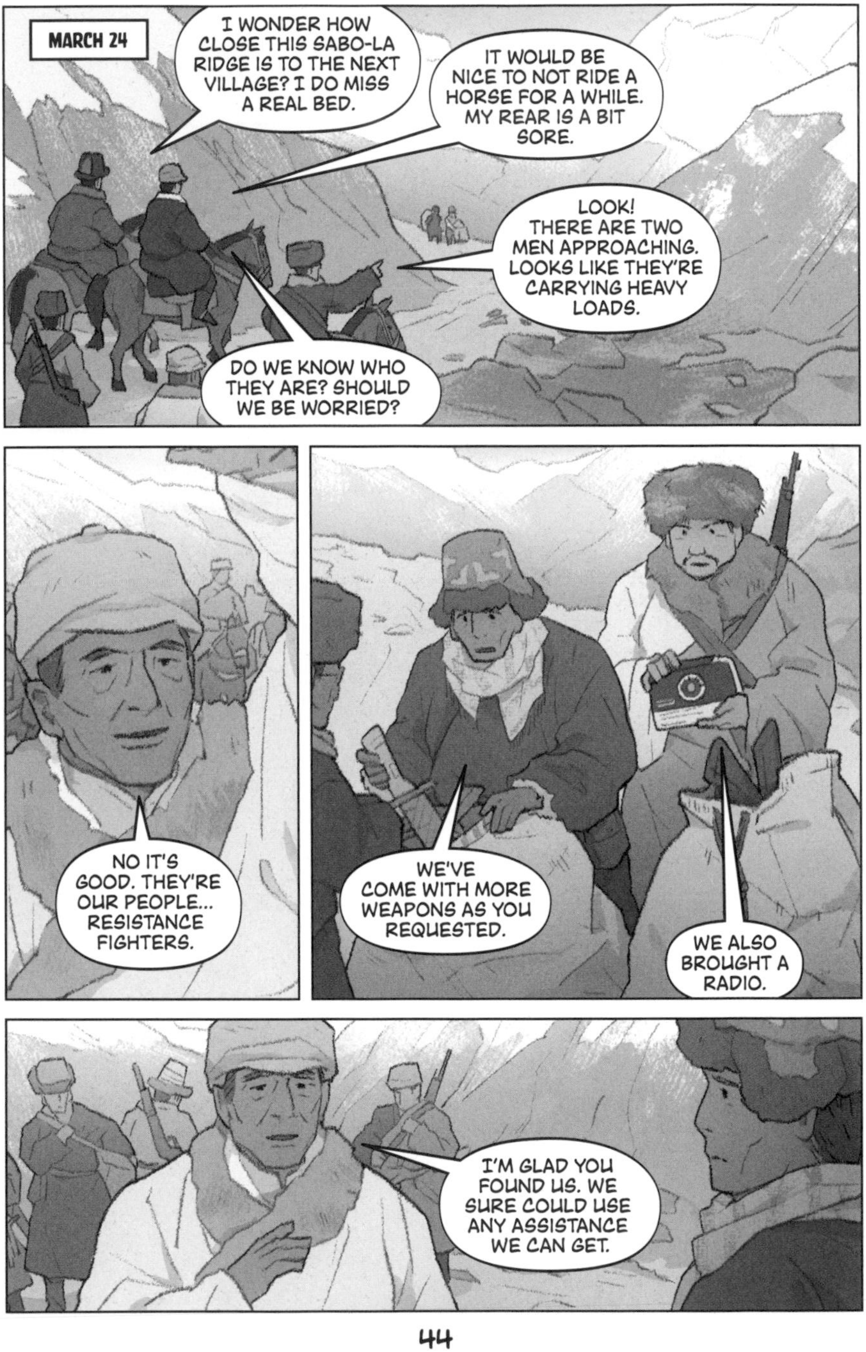
MARCH 24
I WONDER HOW CLOSE THIS SABO-LA RIDGE IS TO THE NEXT VILLAGE? I DO MISS A REAL BED.
IT WOULD BE NICE TO NOT RIDE A HORSE FOR A WHILE. MY REAR IS A BIT SORE.
LOOK! THERE ARE TWO MEN APPROACHING. LOOKS LIKE THEY'RE CARRYING HEAVY LOADS.
DO WE KNOW WHO THEY ARE? SHOULD WE BE WORRIED?
NO IT'S GOOD. THEY'RE OUR PEOPLE... RESISTANCE FIGHTERS.
WE'VE COME WITH MORE WEAPONS AS YOU REQUESTED.
WE ALSO BROUGHT A RADIO.
I'M GLAD YOU FOUND US. WE SURE COULD USE ANY ASSISTANCE WE CAN GET.

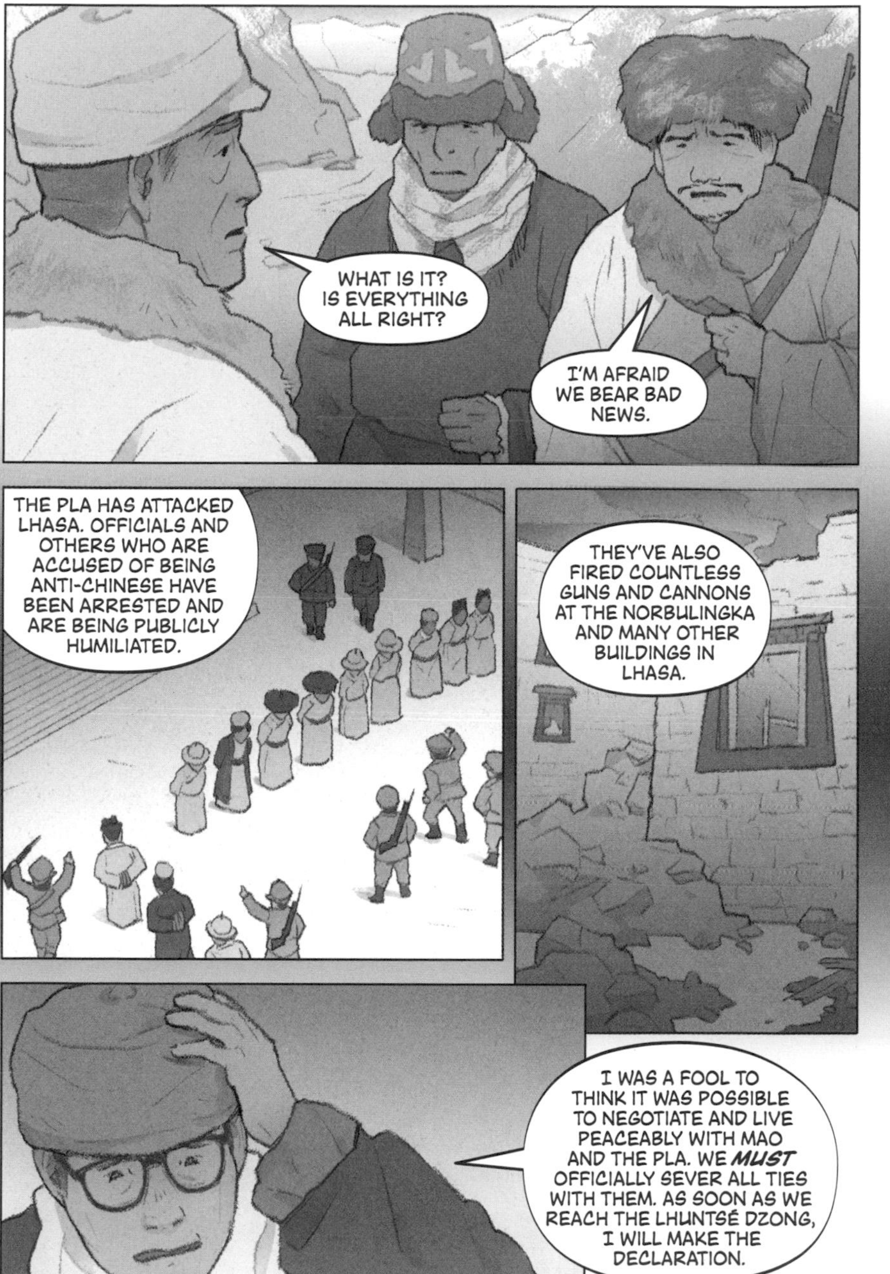
WHAT IS IT? IS EVERYTHING ALL RIGHT?
I'M AFRAID WE BEAR BAD NEWS.
THE PLA HAS ATTACKED LHASA. OFFICIALS AND OTHERS WHO ARE ACCUSED OF BEING ANTI-CHINESE HAVE BEEN ARRESTED AND ARE BEING PUBLICLY HUMILIATED.
THEY'VE ALSO FIRED COUNTLESS GUNS AND CANNONS AT THE NORBULINGKA AND MANY OTHER BUILDINGS IN LHASA.
I WAS A FOOL TO THINK IT WAS POSSIBLE TO NEGOTIATE AND LIVE PEACEABLY WITH MAO AND THE PLA. WE *MUST* OFFICIALLY SEVER ALL TIES WITH THEM. AS SOON AS WE REACH THE LHUNTSÉ DZONG, I WILL MAKE THE DECLARATION.

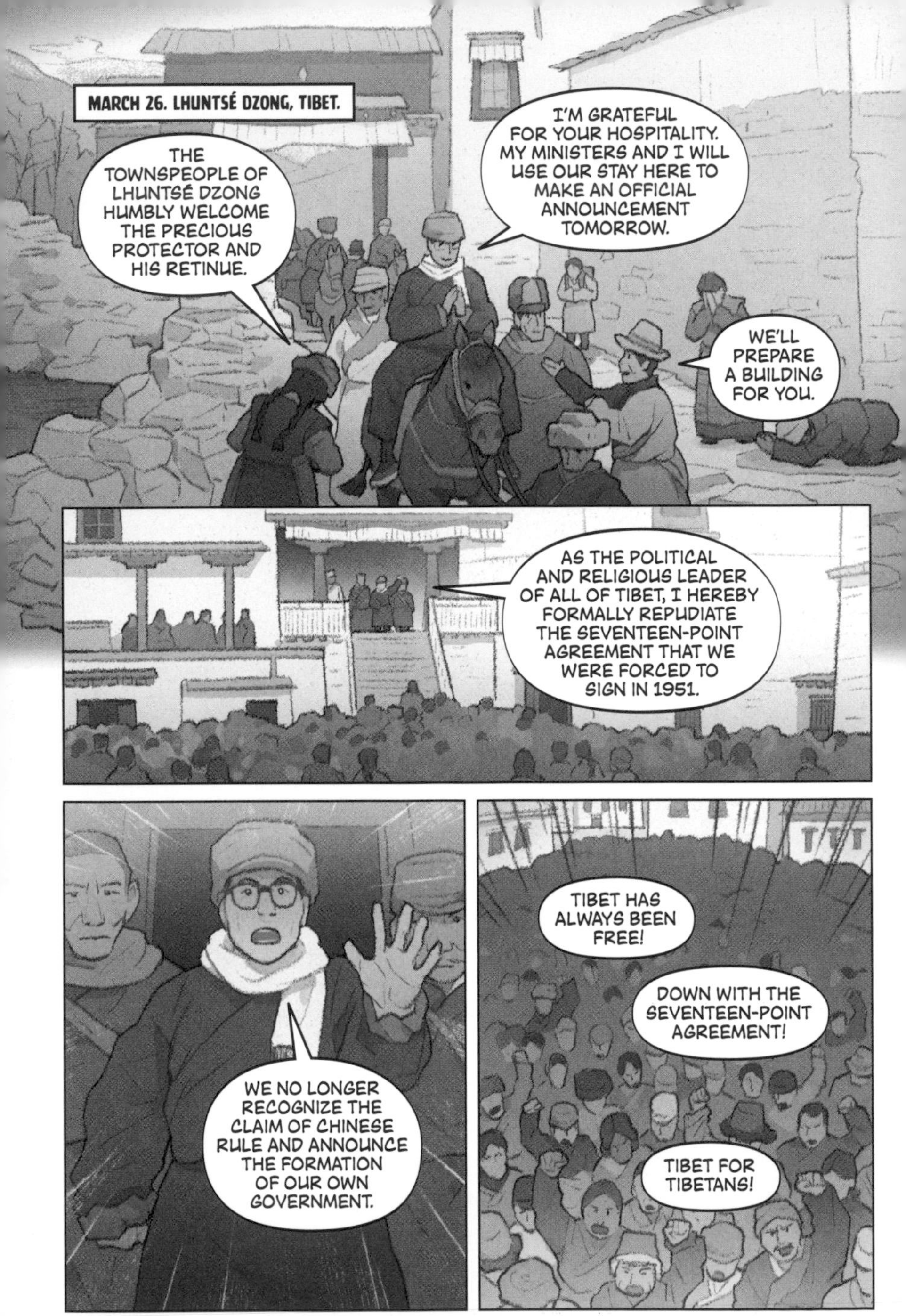
MARCH 26. LHUNTSÉ DZONG, TIBET.
THE TOWNSPEOPLE OF LHUNTSÉ DZONG HUMBLY WELCOME THE PRECIOUS PROTECTOR AND HIS RETINUE.
I'M GRATEFUL FOR YOUR HOSPITALITY. MY MINISTERS AND I WILL USE OUR STAY HERE TO MAKE AN OFFICIAL ANNOUNCEMENT TOMORROW.
WE'LL PREPARE A BUILDING FOR YOU.
AS THE POLITICAL AND RELIGIOUS LEADER OF ALL OF TIBET, I HEREBY FORMALLY REPUDIATE THE SEVENTEEN-POINT AGREEMENT THAT WE WERE FORCED TO SIGN IN 1951.
WE NO LONGER RECOGNIZE THE CLAIM OF CHINESE RULE AND ANNOUNCE THE FORMATION OF OUR OWN GOVERNMENT.
TIBET HAS ALWAYS BEEN FREE!
DOWN WITH THE SEVENTEEN-POINT AGREEMENT!
TIBET FOR TIBETANS!

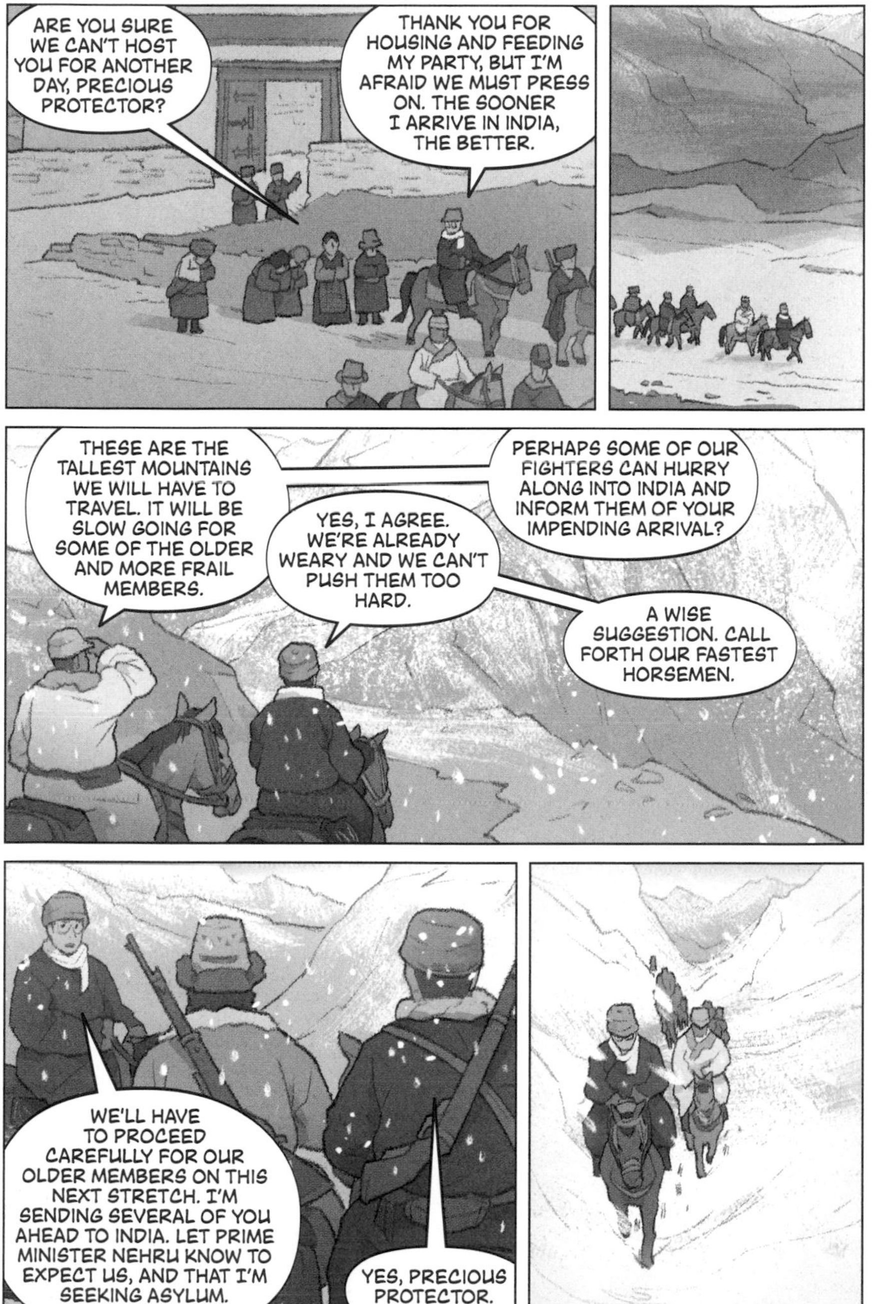
ARE YOU SURE WE CAN'T HOST YOU FOR ANOTHER DAY, PRECIOUS PROTECTOR?
THANK YOU FOR HOUSING AND FEEDING MY PARTY, BUT I'M AFRAID WE MUST PRESS ON. THE SOONER I ARRIVE IN INDIA, THE BETTER.
THESE ARE THE TALLEST MOUNTAINS WE WILL HAVE TO TRAVEL. IT WILL BE SLOW GOING FOR SOME OF THE OLDER AND MORE FRAIL MEMBERS.
YES, I AGREE. WE'RE ALREADY WEARY AND WE CAN'T PUSH THEM TOO HARD.
PERHAPS SOME OF OUR FIGHTERS CAN HURRY ALONG INTO INDIA AND INFORM THEM OF YOUR IMPENDING ARRIVAL?
A WISE SUGGESTION. CALL FORTH OUR FASTEST HORSEMEN.
WE'LL HAVE TO PROCEED CAREFULLY FOR OUR OLDER MEMBERS ON THIS NEXT STRETCH. I'M SENDING SEVERAL OF YOU AHEAD TO INDIA. LET PRIME MINISTER NEHRU KNOW TO EXPECT US, AND THAT I'M SEEKING ASYLUM.
YES, PRECIOUS PROTECTOR.

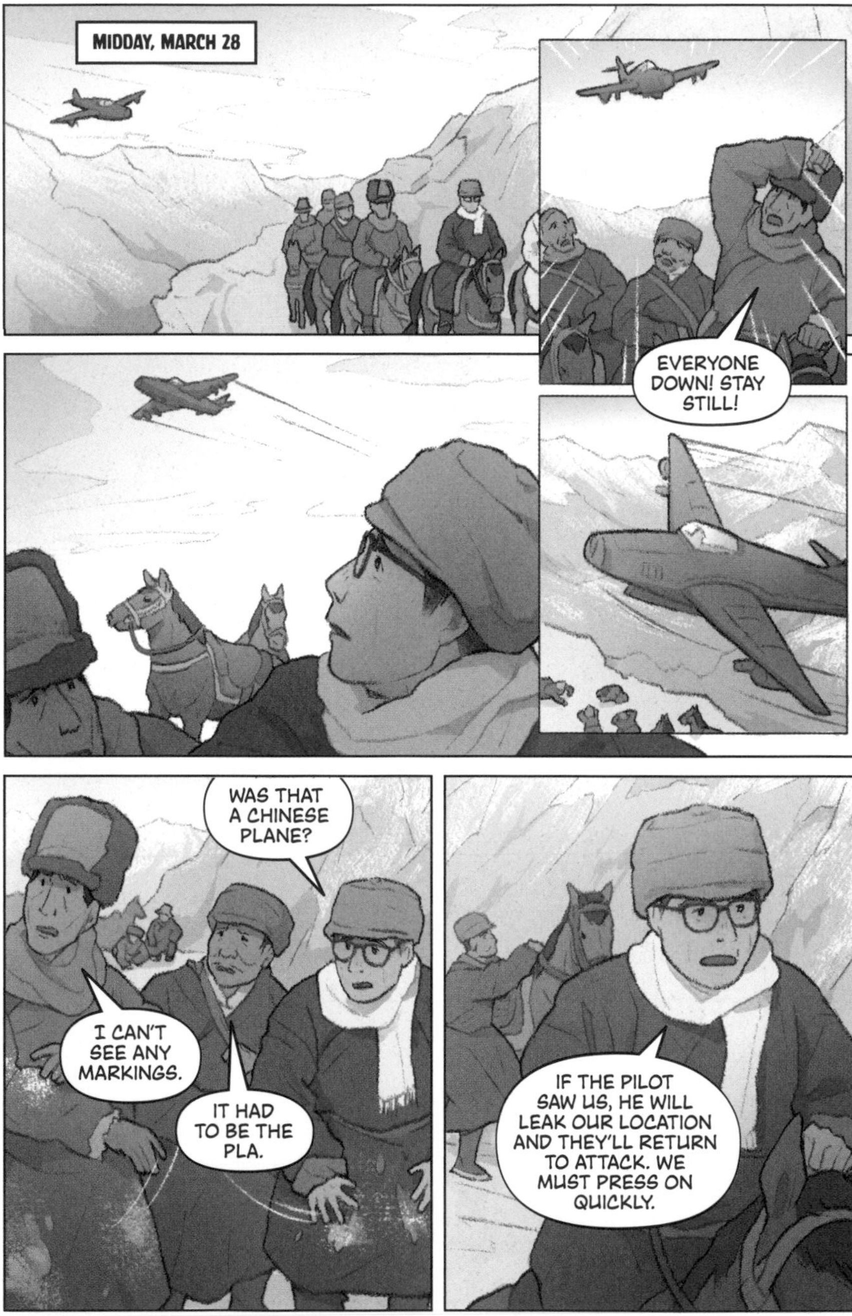
MIDDAY, MARCH 28
EVERYONE DOWN! STAY STILL!
WAS THAT A CHINESE PLANE?
I CAN'T SEE ANY MARKINGS.
IT HAD TO BE THE PLA.
IF THE PILOT SAW US, HE WILL LEAK OUR LOCATION AND THEY'LL RETURN TO ATTACK. WE MUST PRESS ON QUICKLY.

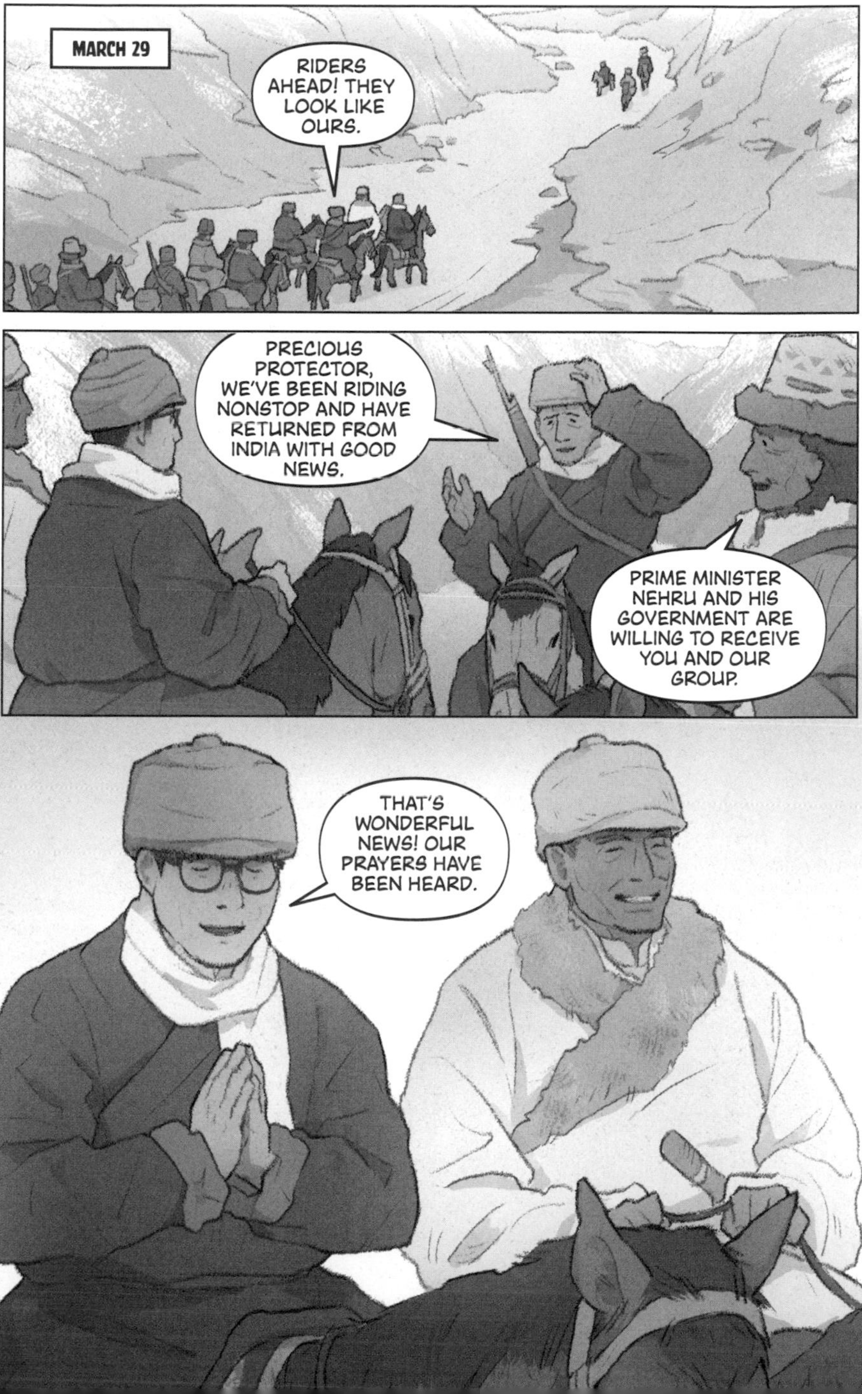
MARCH 29
RIDERS AHEAD! THEY LOOK LIKE OURS.
PRECIOUS PROTECTOR, WE'VE BEEN RIDING NONSTOP AND HAVE RETURNED FROM INDIA WITH GOOD NEWS.
PRIME MINISTER NEHRU AND HIS GOVERNMENT ARE WILLING TO RECEIVE YOU AND OUR GROUP.
THAT'S WONDERFUL NEWS! OUR PRAYERS HAVE BEEN HEARD.

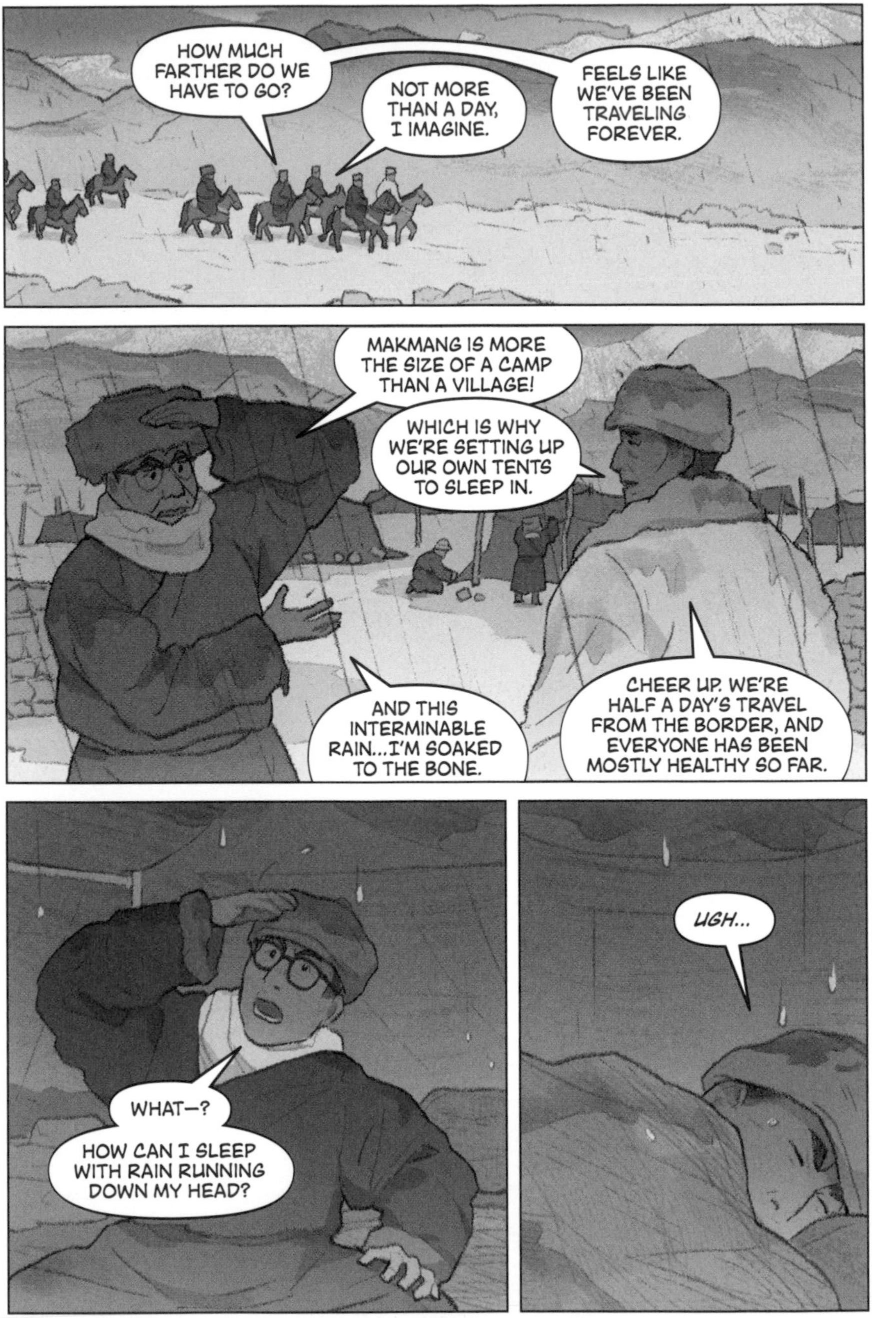
HOW MUCH FARTHER DO WE HAVE TO GO?
NOT MORE THAN A DAY, I IMAGINE.
FEELS LIKE WE'VE BEEN TRAVELING FOREVER.
MAKMANG IS MORE THE SIZE OF A CAMP THAN A VILLAGE!
WHICH IS WHY WE'RE SETTING UP OUR OWN TENTS TO SLEEP IN.
AND THIS INTERMINABLE RAIN...I'M SOAKED TO THE BONE.
CHEER UP. WE'RE HALF A DAY'S TRAVEL FROM THE BORDER, AND EVERYONE HAS BEEN MOSTLY HEALTHY SO FAR.
WHAT—?
HOW CAN I SLEEP WITH RAIN RUNNING DOWN MY HEAD?
UGH...

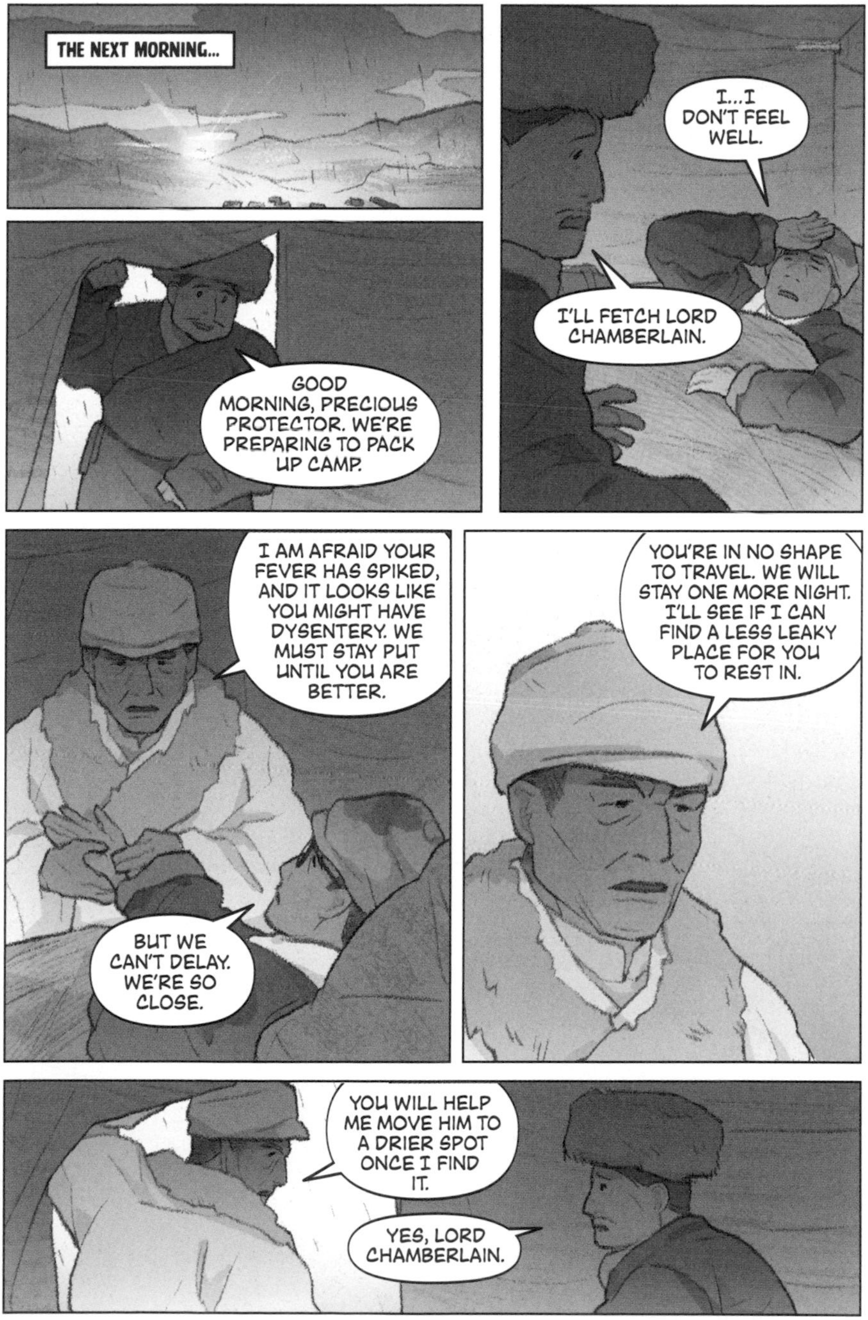
THE NEXT MORNING...
GOOD MORNING, PRECIOUS PROTECTOR. WE'RE PREPARING TO PACK UP CAMP.
I...I DON'T FEEL WELL.
I'LL FETCH LORD CHAMBERLAIN.
I AM AFRAID YOUR FEVER HAS SPIKED, AND IT LOOKS LIKE YOU MIGHT HAVE DYSENTERY. WE MUST STAY PUT UNTIL YOU ARE BETTER.
BUT WE CAN'T DELAY. WE'RE SO CLOSE.
YOU'RE IN NO SHAPE TO TRAVEL. WE WILL STAY ONE MORE NIGHT. I'LL SEE IF I CAN FIND A LESS LEAKY PLACE FOR YOU TO REST IN.
YOU WILL HELP ME MOVE HIM TO A DRIER SPOT ONCE I FIND IT.
YES, LORD CHAMBERLAIN.

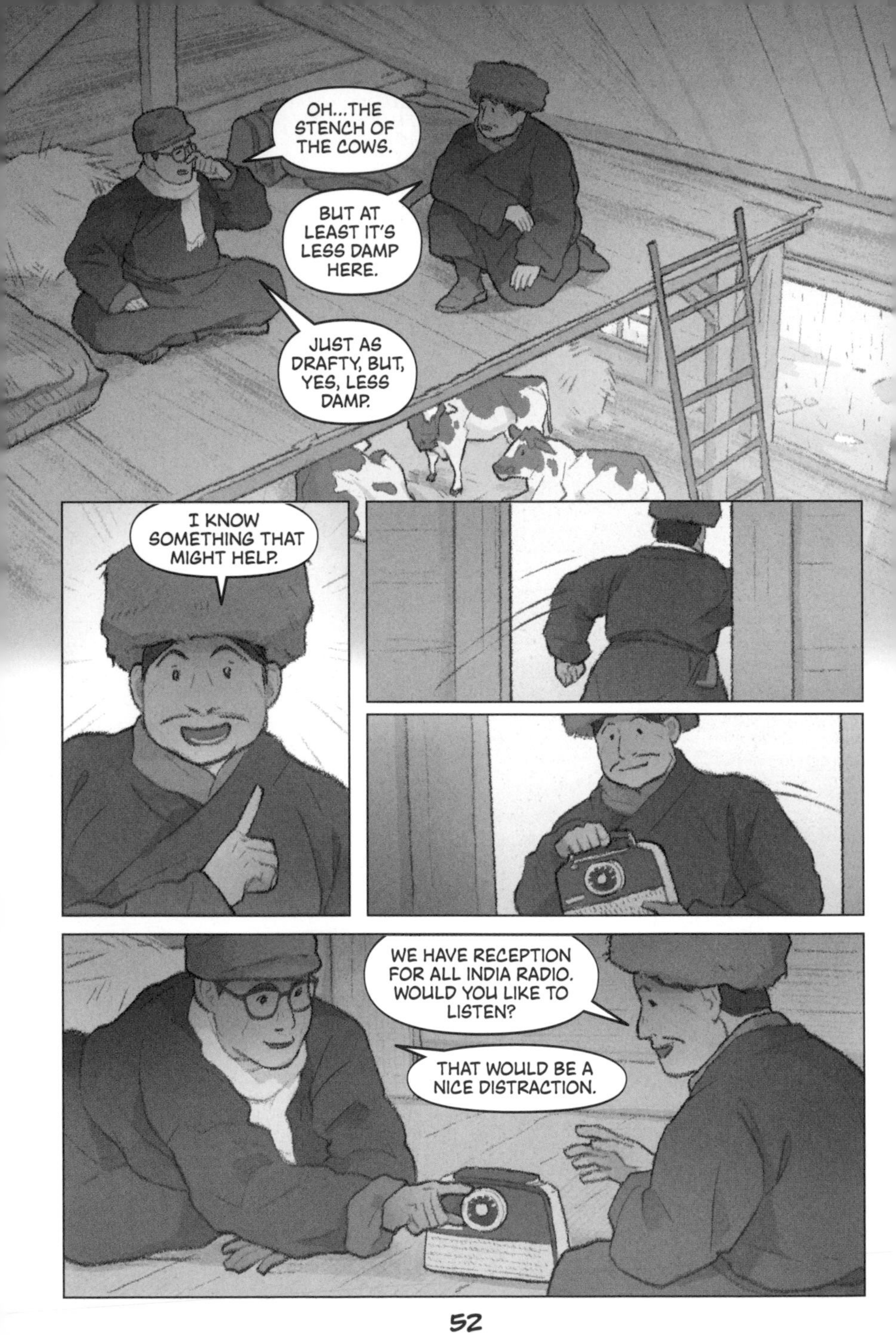
OH...THE STENCH OF THE COWS.
BUT AT LEAST IT'S LESS DAMP HERE.
JUST AS DRAFTY, BUT, YES, LESS DAMP.
I KNOW SOMETHING THAT MIGHT HELP.
WE HAVE RECEPTION FOR ALL INDIA RADIO. WOULD YOU LIKE TO LISTEN?
THAT WOULD BE A NICE DISTRACTION.

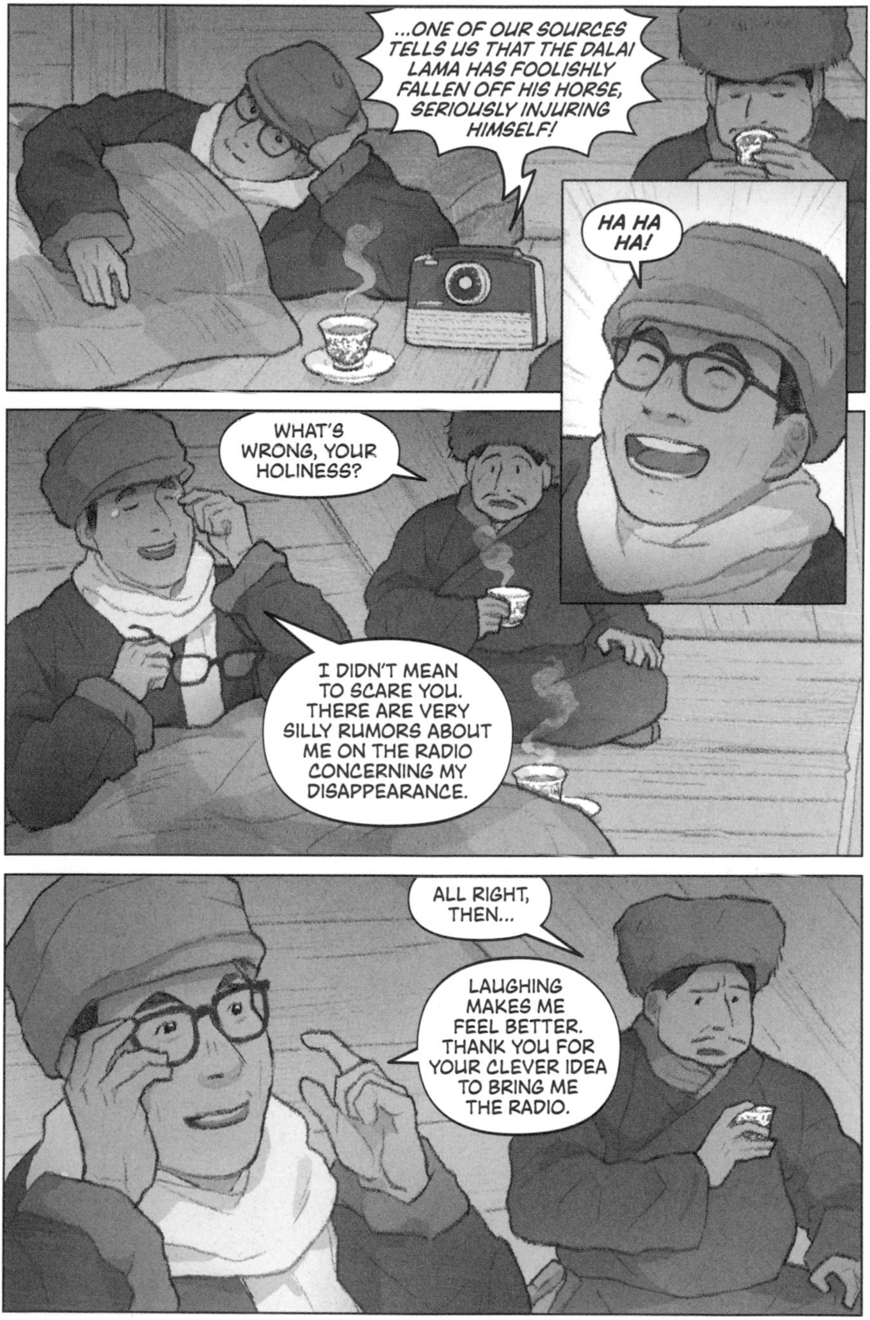
...ONE OF OUR SOURCES TELLS US THAT THE DALAI LAMA HAS FOOLISHLY FALLEN OFF HIS HORSE, SERIOUSLY INJURING HIMSELF!
HA HA HA!
WHAT'S WRONG, YOUR HOLINESS?
I DIDN'T MEAN TO SCARE YOU. THERE ARE VERY SILLY RUMORS ABOUT ME ON THE RADIO CONCERNING MY DISAPPEARANCE.
ALL RIGHT, THEN...
LAUGHING MAKES ME FEEL BETTER. THANK YOU FOR YOUR CLEVER IDEA TO BRING ME THE RADIO.

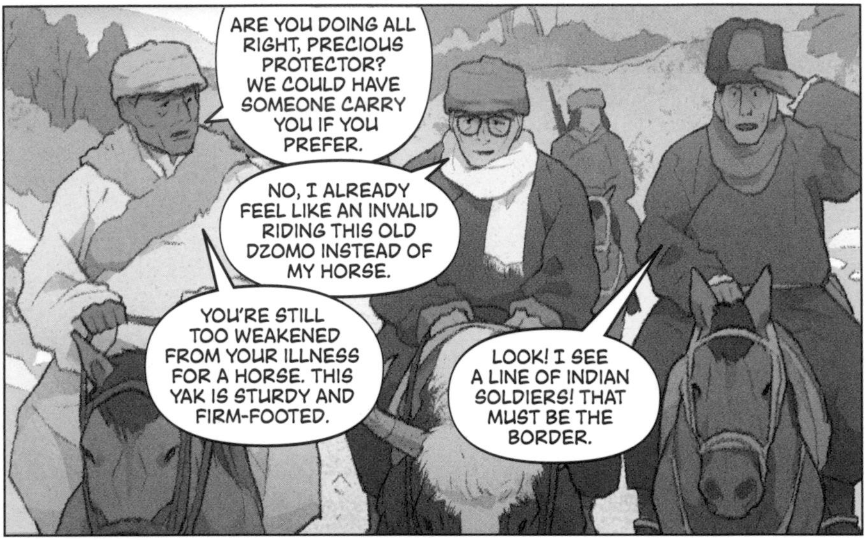
ARE YOU DOING ALL RIGHT, PRECIOUS PROTECTOR? WE COULD HAVE SOMEONE CARRY YOU IF YOU PREFER.
NO, I ALREADY FEEL LIKE AN INVALID RIDING THIS OLD DZOMO INSTEAD OF MY HORSE.
YOU'RE STILL TOO WEAKENED FROM YOUR ILLNESS FOR A HORSE. THIS YAK IS STURDY AND FIRM-FOOTED.
LOOK! I SEE A LINE OF INDIAN SOLDIERS! THAT MUST BE THE BORDER.

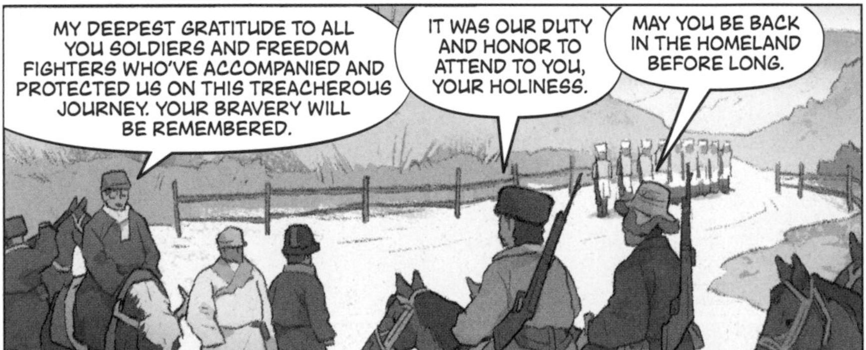
MY DEEPEST GRATITUDE TO ALL YOU SOLDIERS AND FREEDOM FIGHTERS WHO'VE ACCOMPANIED AND PROTECTED US ON THIS TREACHEROUS JOURNEY. YOUR BRAVERY WILL BE REMEMBERED.
IT WAS OUR DUTY AND HONOR TO ATTEND TO YOU, YOUR HOLINESS.
MAY YOU BE BACK IN THE HOMELAND BEFORE LONG.

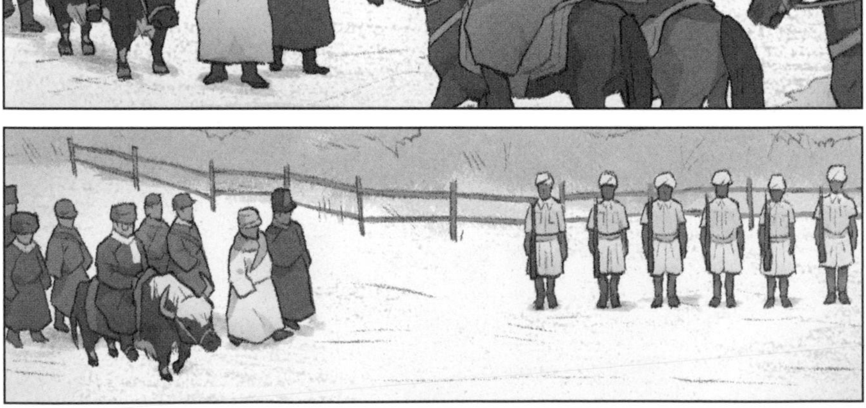

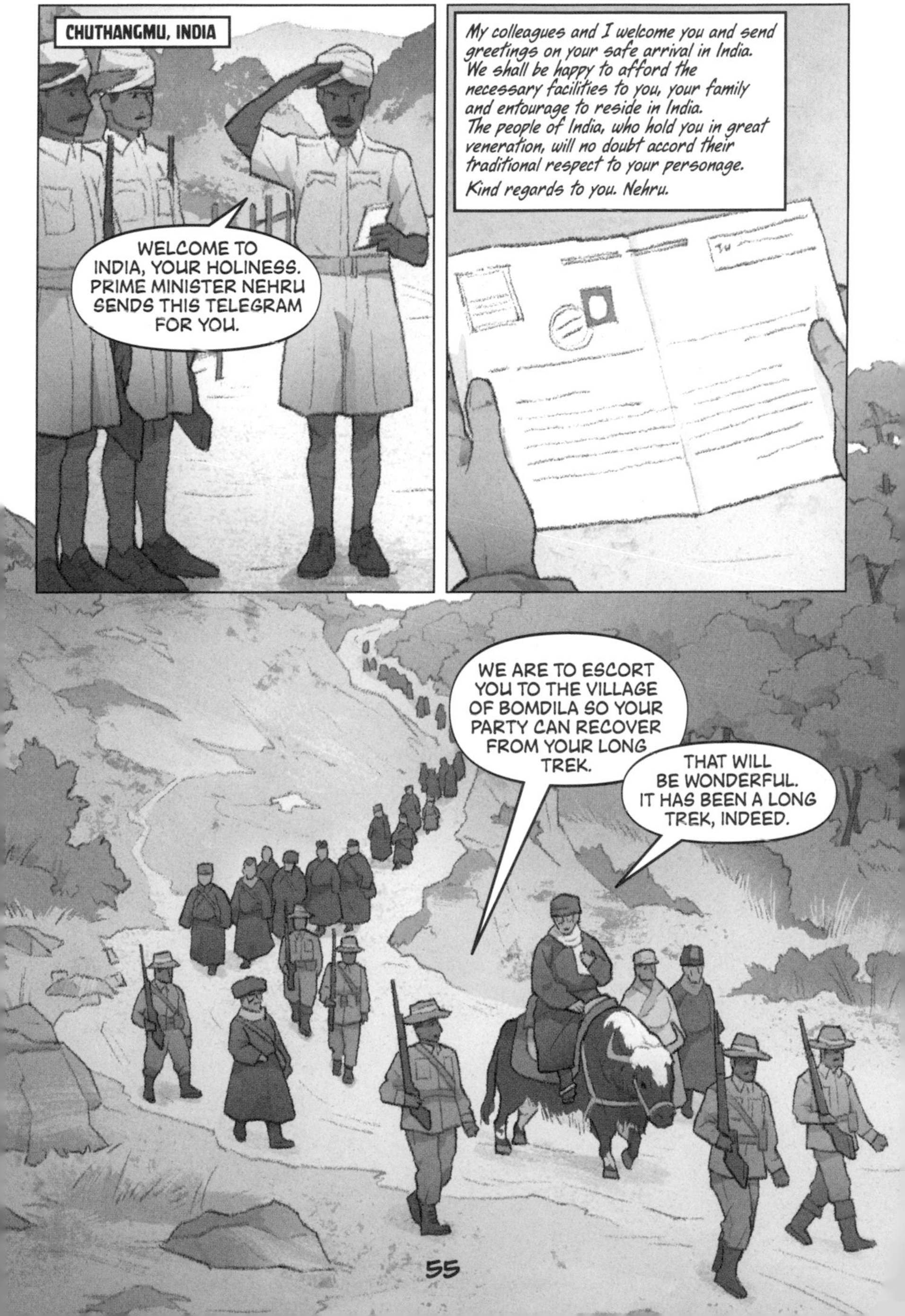
CHUTHANGMU, INDIA
WELCOME TO INDIA, YOUR HOLINESS. PRIME MINISTER NEHRU SENDS THIS TELEGRAM FOR YOU.
My colleagues and I welcome you and send greetings on your safe arrival in India. We shall be happy to afford the necessary facilities to you, your family and entourage to reside in India. The people of India, who hold you in great veneration, will no doubt accord their traditional respect to your personage.
Kind regards to you. Nehru.
WE ARE TO ESCORT YOU TO THE VILLAGE OF BOMDILA SO YOUR PARTY CAN RECOVER FROM YOUR LONG TREK.
THAT WILL BE WONDERFUL. IT HAS BEEN A LONG TREK, INDEED.

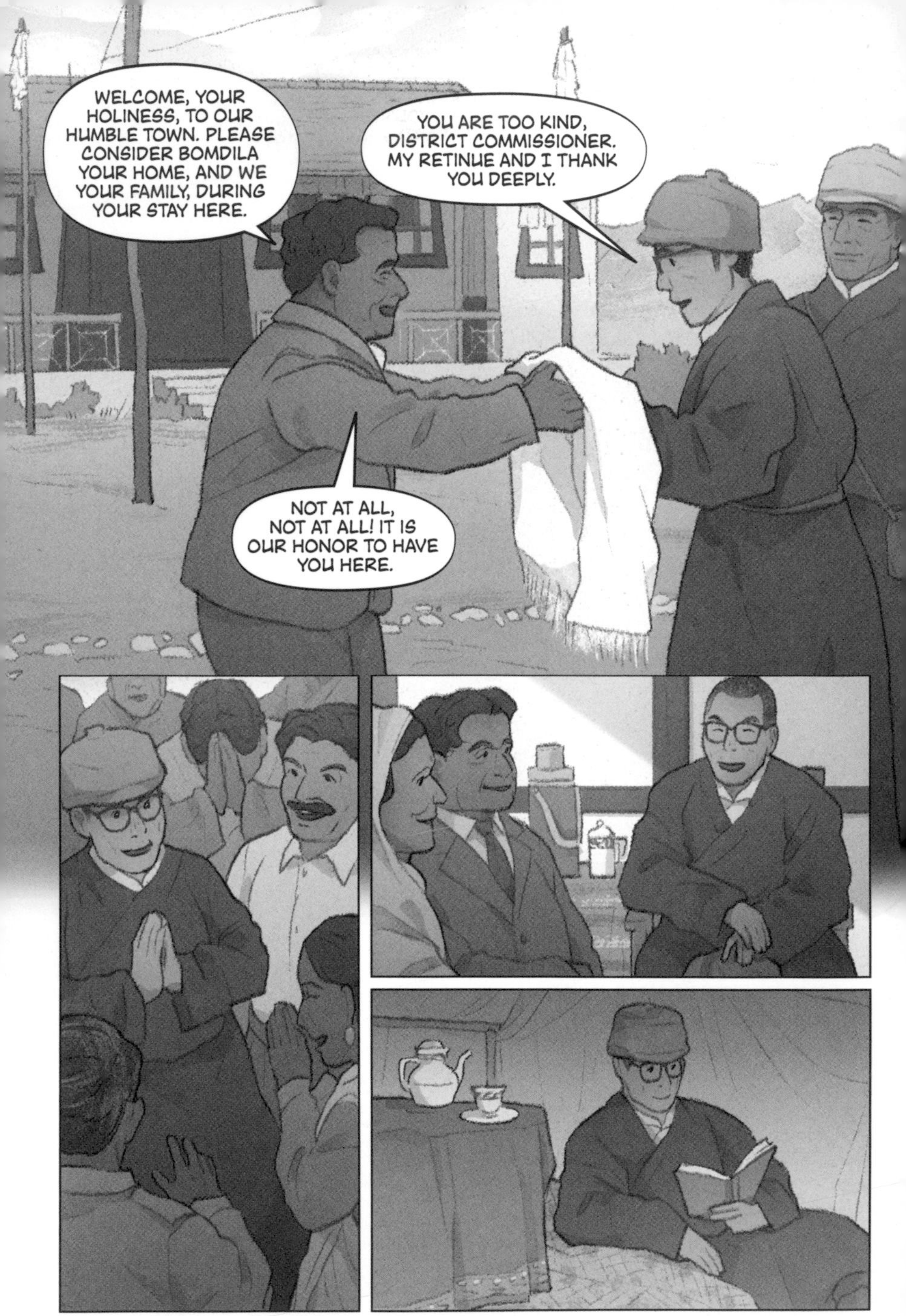
WELCOME, YOUR HOLINESS, TO OUR HUMBLE TOWN. PLEASE CONSIDER BOMDILA YOUR HOME, AND WE YOUR FAMILY, DURING YOUR STAY HERE.
YOU ARE TOO KIND, DISTRICT COMMISSIONER. MY RETINUE AND I THANK YOU DEEPLY.
NOT AT ALL, NOT AT ALL! IT IS OUR HONOR TO HAVE YOU HERE.

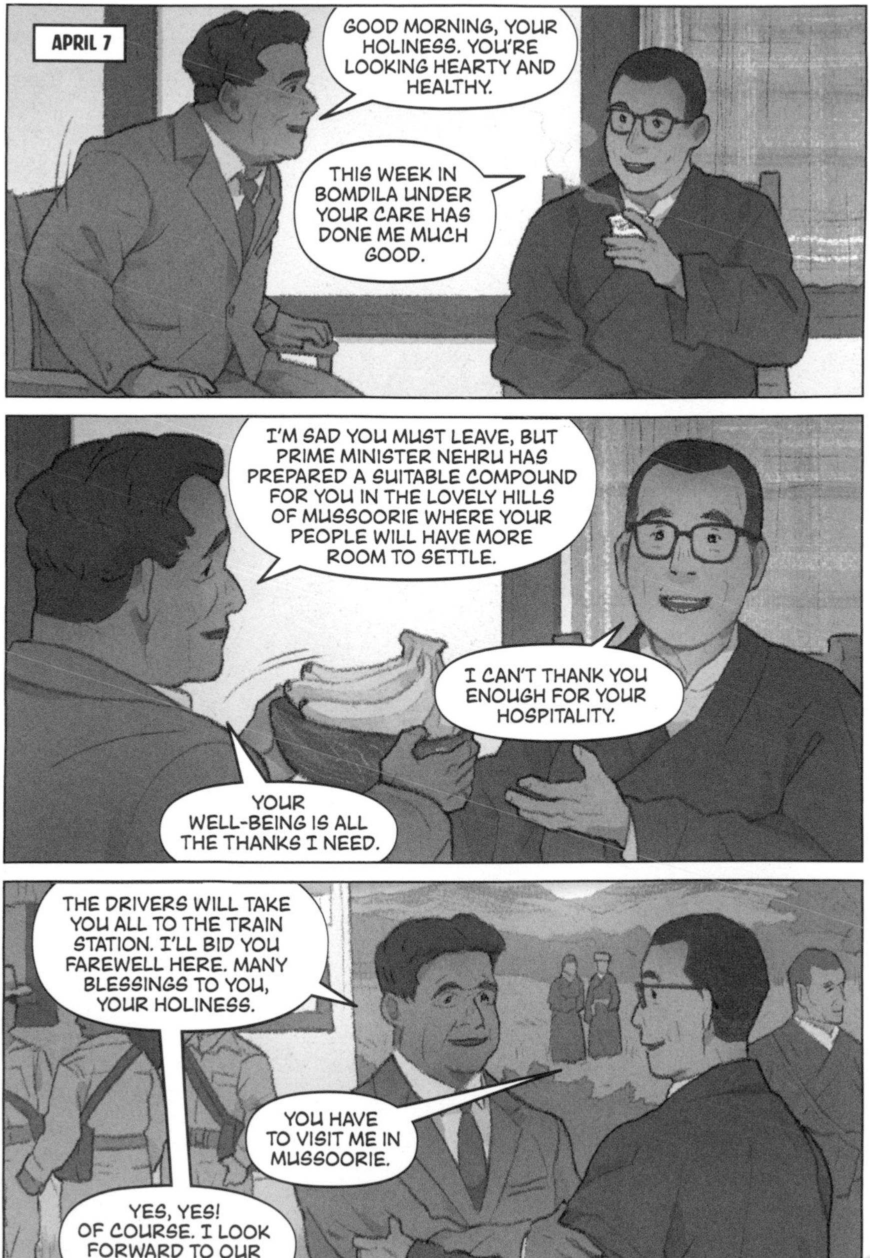
APRIL 7
GOOD MORNING, YOUR HOLINESS. YOU'RE LOOKING HEARTY AND HEALTHY.
THIS WEEK IN BOMDILA UNDER YOUR CARE HAS DONE ME MUCH GOOD.
I'M SAD YOU MUST LEAVE, BUT PRIME MINISTER NEHRU HAS PREPARED A SUITABLE COMPOUND FOR YOU IN THE LOVELY HILLS OF MUSSOORIE WHERE YOUR PEOPLE WILL HAVE MORE ROOM TO SETTLE.
I CAN'T THANK YOU ENOUGH FOR YOUR HOSPITALITY.
YOUR WELL-BEING IS ALL THE THANKS I NEED.
THE DRIVERS WILL TAKE YOU ALL TO THE TRAIN STATION. I'LL BID YOU FAREWELL HERE. MANY BLESSINGS TO YOU, YOUR HOLINESS.
YOU HAVE TO VISIT ME IN MUSSOORIE.
YES, YES! OF COURSE. I LOOK FORWARD TO OUR NEXT MEETING.

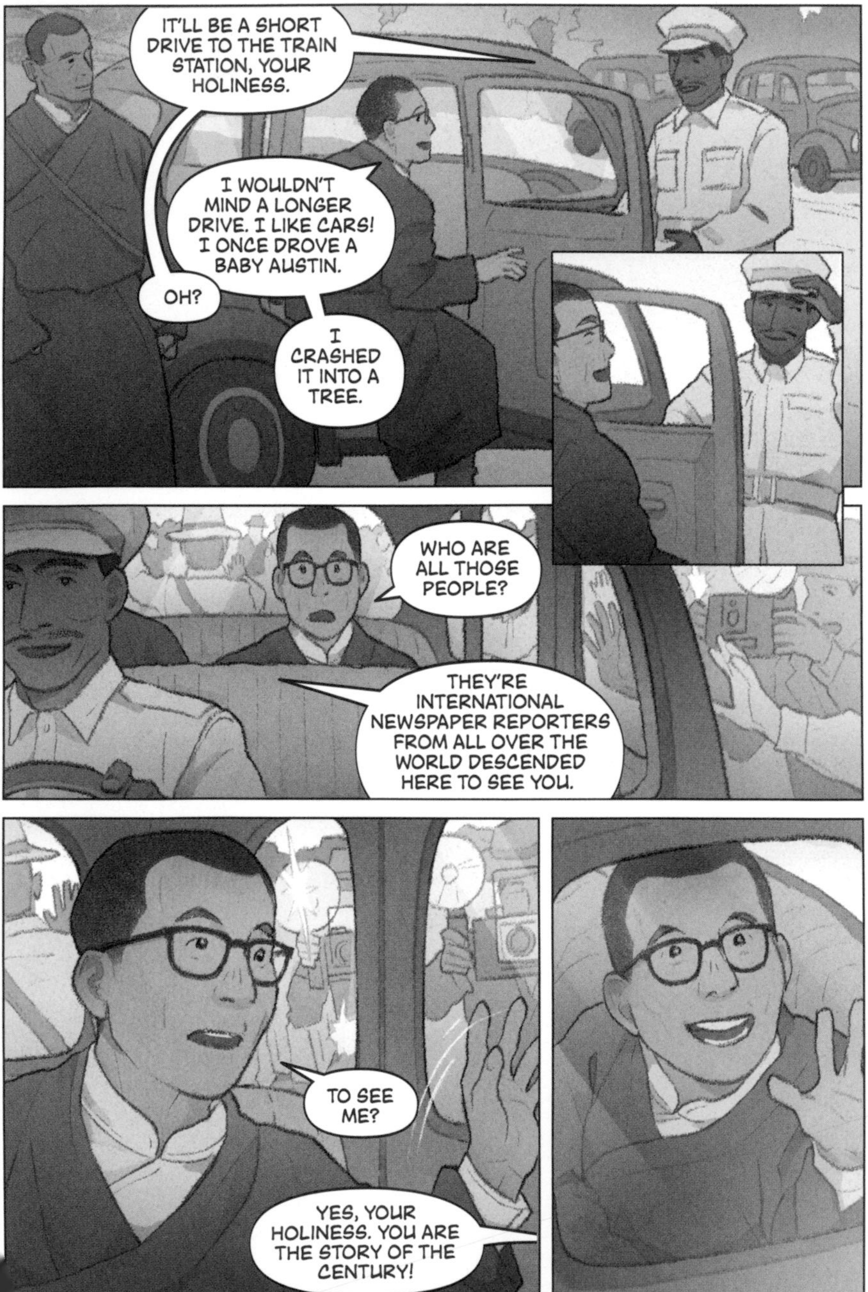
IT'LL BE A SHORT DRIVE TO THE TRAIN STATION, YOUR HOLINESS.
I WOULDN'T MIND A LONGER DRIVE. I LIKE CARS! I ONCE DROVE A BABY AUSTIN.
OH?
I CRASHED IT INTO A TREE.
WHO ARE ALL THOSE PEOPLE?
THEY'RE INTERNATIONAL NEWSPAPER REPORTERS FROM ALL OVER THE WORLD DESCENDED HERE TO SEE YOU.
TO SEE ME?
YES, YOUR HOLINESS. YOU ARE THE STORY OF THE CENTURY!

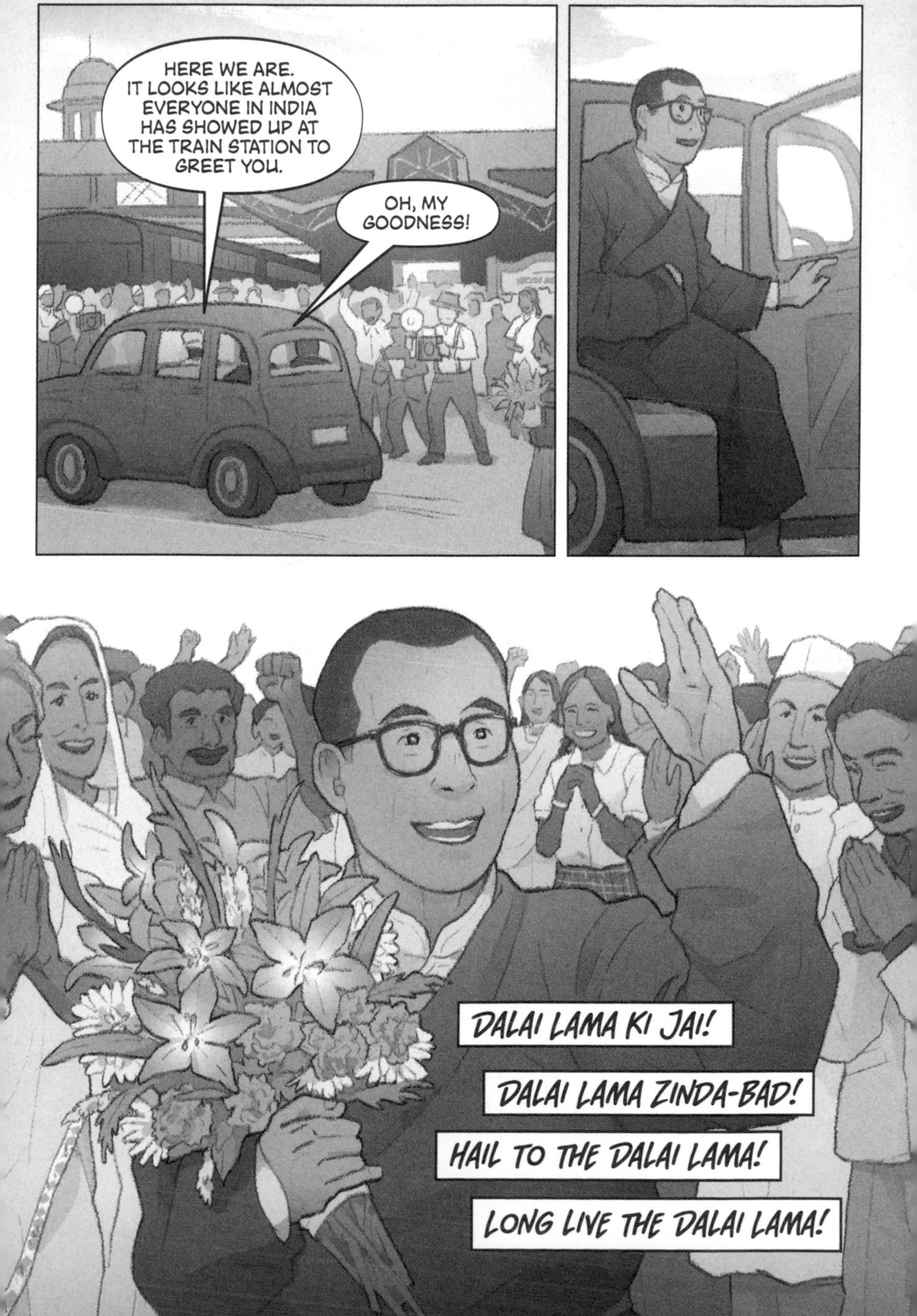

HERE WE ARE. IT LOOKS LIKE ALMOST EVERYONE IN INDIA HAS SHOWED UP AT THE TRAIN STATION TO GREET YOU.
OH, MY GOODNESS!
DALAI LAMA KI JAI!
DALAI LAMA ZINDA-BAD!
HAIL TO THE DALAI LAMA!
LONG LIVE THE DALAI LAMA!

Conclusion

The people of India welcomed the Dalai Lama as an honored guest and gave him a new home. He and his group settled first in Mussoorie, then permanently in Dharamsala, India, where tens of thousands more Tibetans joined them, fleeing from persecution back in their home country. Without the Dalai Lama in Tibet, life became very harsh for Tibetans who remained behind. They were, and still are, subjected to violence, starvation, and public humiliation by the Chinese government.

Dharamsala became the headquarters of the Dalai Lama's exiled government. He drafted a new constitution with laws appropriate to their adopted home and situation. His goal was to establish a democratically elected government for Tibetans, something that Tibet had never had before. The Dalai Lama realized the plan's success depended on educating his people, both to learn about the wider world and to remember their own culture. So, he founded a school which taught Tibetan language, dance, and music, along with regular subjects like math, social studies, and science.

During the 1970s, the Dalai Lama traveled to Europe, the United States, and Canada. Later, he would journey even farther. Not only did he want to experience the world firsthand, but he also wanted to spread word about the challenges Tibet faced under hostile foreign rule. Everywhere he went, he shared his Buddhist philosophy of nonviolent protest and kindness. This philosophy is embodied in one of his favorite prayers:

For as long as space endures,
And for as long as living beings remain,
Until then may I, too, abide
To dispel the misery of the world.

Because of his tireless efforts, the Dalai Lama and Tibet are now internationally known. In 1989, when he was fifty-four years old, he was awarded the Nobel Peace Prize for his work and his message of peace.

The fateful decision to escape in March 1959 made a world of difference—and a difference to the world.

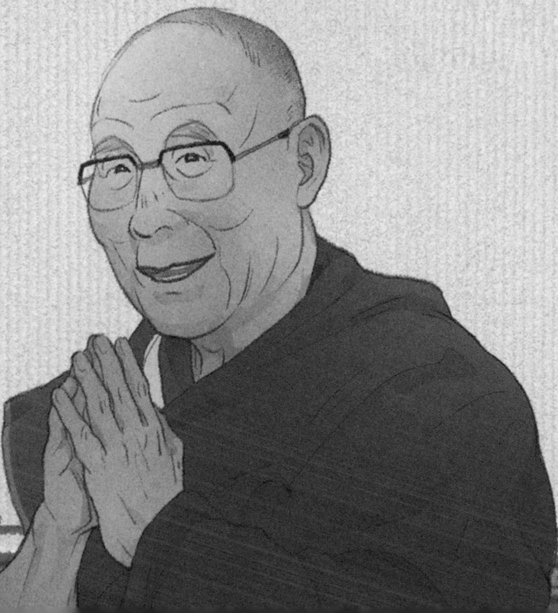

Timeline of the 14th Dalai Lama's Life

1935 — The Dalai Lama is born on July 6 in the small village of Takster, Tibet, and named Lhamo Thondup

1939 — Arrives on October 8 in Lhasa with his family after being proclaimed the 14th Dalai Lama

1940 — Officially enthroned as the Dalai Lama on February 22

1950 — China's People's Liberation Army invades Tibet on October 7

1951 — The Seventeen-Point Agreement is signed on May 23

1959 — Protests erupt against China's People's Liberation Army, as the army begins to attack villages in Tibet

— The Dalai Lama flees the country

— Crosses into India on March 31

1960 — Settles in Dharamsala, India, on April 30, where he establishes a school and a new Tibetan government

1987 — Puts forth the Five-Point Peace Plan to the US Congress's Human Rights Caucus, on September 21, addressing how to establish protections for Tibet

1989 — Selected to receive the Nobel Peace Prize in October "for advocating peaceful solutions based upon tolerance and mutual respect in order to preserve the historical and cultural heritage of his people"

2011 — Steps down as the political leader of Tibet on March 19

Bibliography

*Books for young readers

Ginsburgs, George, and Michael Mathos. "Tibet's Administration in the Transition Period, 1951–1954." *Pacific Affairs*, vol. 32, no. 2 (1959): 162–177. https://doi.org/10.2307/2753562.v.

Gyatso, Tenzin. *Freedom in Exile: The Autobiography of the Dalai Lama*. New York: HarperCollins, 1990.

Norman, Alexander. *The Dalai Lama: An Extraordinary Life*. Boston: Houghton Mifflin Harcourt, 2020.

*Rau, Dana Meachen. *Who Is the Dalai Lama?* New York: Penguin Workshop, 2018.

Tethong, Tenzin Geyche, and Gautam Pemmaraju. *His Holiness the Fourteenth Dalai Lama: An Illustrated Biography*. Northampton, MA: Interlink Books, 2021.

Website

www.dalailama.com

ABOUT THE CREATORS

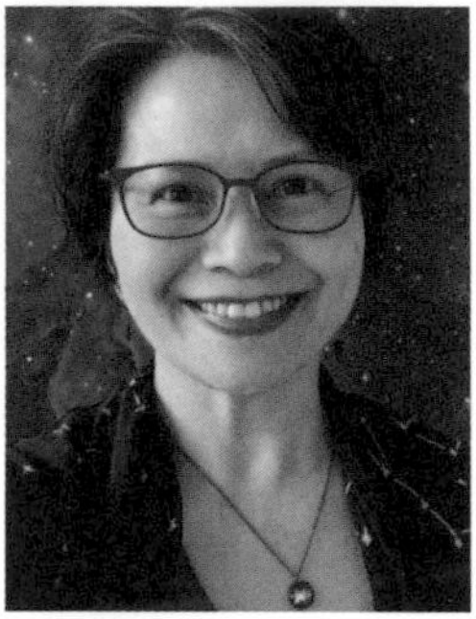

Teresa Robeson is the APALA Award-winning author of *Queen of Physics: How Wu Chien Shiung Helped Unlock the Secrets of the Atom* (also ILA Nonfiction Picture Book Honor and NCTE Orbis Pictus Nonfiction Recommended Book). Other publications include *Two Bicycles in Beijing* and an essay in *Nonfiction Writers Dig Deep*, edited by Melissa Stewart. Teresa lives with her scientist-professor husband, younger son, and a motley crew of chickens on their twenty-seven-acre mini homestead. Learn more about her work at teresarobeson.com.

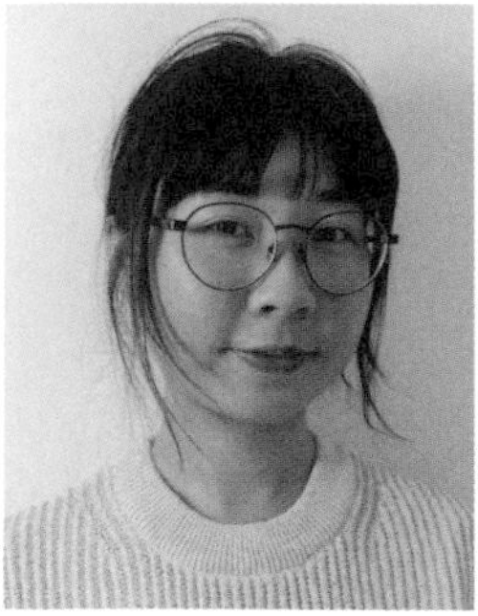

Angela Poon is a freelance illustrator and comic artist living in Mississauga, Ontario. She is a graduate of Sheridan College's Bachelor of Illustration program, and is the illustrator of Deborah Kerbel's graphic novel *Fred & Marjorie: A Doctor, a Dog, and the Discovery of Insulin*. Angela enjoys capturing warmth and little moments of everyday life in her illustrations. Find more of her work at angela-poon.com.